this book is about sex

by tucker shaw and fiona gibb

AlloyBooks

Dedication:

Tucker:
To Jennifer T., who knows that a sense of humor is the most important thing in the world.

Fiona:
To my parents, for having sex in the first place.

Thanks to:
Matt Diamond, Jim Johnson, and Sam Gradess for the opportunity;
Susan Kaplow for the vision;
Jodi Anderson for the way she rules;
Angie Maximo, Lauren Goodman, and Jodi Smith for the skills;
Russell Gordon, Lauren Monchik, and Marci Senders for the look;
Everyone at 17th Street Productions and Penguin Putnam for making it all happen;
and most of all, the Alloy.com community for the inspiration.

ALLOY BOOKS
Published by the Penguin Group
Penguin Putnam Books for Young Readers,
345 Hudson Street, New York, New York 10014, U.S.A.

Published by Puffin Books,
a division of Penguin Putnam Books for Young Readers, 2000

10 9 8 7 6 5 4 3 2 1

Cover design by Russell Gordon
Interior design by Lauren Monchik
Interior illustrations by Marci Senders

Produced by 17th Street Productions,
an Alloy Online, Inc. company
33 West 17th Street
New York, NY 10011

ISBN 0-14-130920-2
Printed in the United States of America

table of contents

1. the **first** time   2

2. it takes two   18

3. sex and your social life   48

4. sex 411   72

5. protection and STDs   90

6. masturbation   116

7. pregnancy   124

8. same sex stuff   140

9. sex and your family   156

introduction

Odds are, you think about sex a lot. And if our experience as sex experts at Alloy.com is any indication, that is pretty normal. We get hundreds of questions about sex every day from people all over the map. Some questions are easy, like, "Will masturbating affect the size of my penis?" (page 120). Some are much tougher, like, "What can I expect if I have an abortion?" (page 134). But all of them are real questions from people in need of real answers.

The thing is, no matter how much everybody thinks about sex, hardly anyone really talks about it. And the people who are talking about it are often trying to impress you, or telling you what they think you want to hear. So for the most part, sex is still kind of a mystery. Which is where we come in.

Now, we're not from the school of talking about sex nonstop, but we're not about ignoring it, either. What we *are* about is listening to your questions, hearing your concerns, and doing our best to help you out. So we've packed this book with all the sex advice you've asked for. And we've included lots of funky odds and ends and advice from teens like you.

This book won't answer every sex question in the world. But it will shed a little light on some of the biggies. So have fun with it. Learn from it. And hey! Let's be careful out there.

tucker and fiona

the first time

For people who are actually having it, sex can be a huge mystery. And if you're still a virgin, you've got even more unanswered questions. So in this chapter, we're going to demystify the mystery that is "the first time." Why it's such a big deal, whether or not you should do it, and when's the right time.

Now, we can't give you 100 percent definitive answers to any of these questions. Because when it comes to making decisions about whether or not to do it, it really all comes down to you and your situation, how old you are, what your religious and personal beliefs are, who you're with and what you expect from that person, and what you're ready for emotionally.

With all that said, my best advice is this: Don't lose your virginity until you know you're ready for it—and all the complications and consequences that come with it. That means not having sex because everyone else is, because you feel pressured, or because you just want to get it over with.

And if you do decide you're ready for sex, remember: your first time doesn't define your sex life forever. You'll have the rest of your life to have sex. And it almost always gets better with time.

fiona

why is **virginity**
such a big deal❓

I'm a virgin, and I guess I'll stay one for a long time. My question: Why does everyone value virginity so much? Why is it so important? And why do people regret losing it so much? What's up with that?　　　　　—DAVE

DEAR DAVE,

I guess virginity is a big deal because, as human beings, sex in general is a big deal.

I mean, think about it. Your sex drive is a huge part of who you are. And it impacts your whole, entire life—for better or for worse. So the first time you do it, it's major.

Also, having sex takes two people, and the first time you do it, you're showing someone a part of yourself that you've never shown anyone before. Not just literally showing them your privates, but really exposing yourself emotionally, too.

People talk about virginity a lot. Some people judge you based on it. Some people see it as something that separates the kids from the grown-ups. Some people divide the world into virgins and nonvirgins. Your status plays a major part in your relationships.

But remember this: All the pressure and stuff in the world can't change the fact that you're still you, whether it's the virgin you or the nonvirgin you.

ARE YOU A VIRGIN?
Yes: 54%
No: 42%
No answer: 4%

 You know, I am so glad I never did it with someone I had lukewarm feel-

fiona says

Okay, so here comes my attempt at a major answer. . . . I think virginity has such significance in our culture mostly because it's always been that way. See, back in the olden days, virginity was literally a commodity because it was wrapped up in reproduction. A man wanted to be sure that he "owned" the virginity of his mate because in that way he "owned" that woman's potential for offspring. Women of marrying age were seen as damaged goods if they didn't have their virginity intact—women who weren't "pure" ended up single—or worse. Losing it truly meant losing her self-worth. (In many parts of the world, the situation is still the same.)

But for men, of course, it was the other way around—by having sex with a virgin, they were gaining something of value.

Now, to me, that seems like a pretty unfair double standard. Luckily, it's changing, thanks to the sexual revolution, birth control, and a host of other factors. If you ask me, this is a good thing—because there's much more to a person's identity than whether or not they've had sex. I mean, isn't that kind of a random thing to put so much emphasis on?

I think so.

Sex should be reserved for the wedding night. . . . I mean, what an awesome wedding present to give your guy! —Me

I lost my virginity about a month ago, and I don't understand why people look down on me. . . . I am still the same person as I was before. —Lystra

ings for.—Alicia Silverstone in *Clueless* It is one of the superstitions of

am i a virgin?

There's a lot you can do sexually without actually having sex. But once you cross the line, there's no going back. According to Tucker and Fiona, here's how to know when you're technically still a virgin.

Given manual sex (given a hand job or fingered someone) . . .YES

Received manual sex (been given a hand job or been fingered by someone) . . .YES

Given oral sex . . .YES

Received oral sex . . .YES

Had dry sex (no penetration) with or without clothes on . . .YES

Had anal sex . . .NO

Had vaginal sex . . .NO

Had vaginal sex—but just for a minute . . .NO

i'm **embarrassed**
to do it

I have been going out with my BF for almost a year, and I think that I'm ready to have sex with him. But the problem is that I'm, like, really embarrassed about it!!! I mean, I can't help that I think like that, but whenever I think about it, it just makes me feel so embarrassed!! I really need some comforting advice.
Thanks a lot.   —EMBARRASSED

HEY, EMBARRASSED,

I know what you mean. Think about it . . . You get all butt naked, then roll around, then you have to put that thing all up in there. You start sayin' things that don't make sense. Then there's all those noises your body makes. Not to mention the stickiness. Face it—the whole experience is really hilarious.

Luckily, everyone involved is in the same boat.

Yep. As embarrassed as you are, your boyfriend may be just as freaked. Except being a guy and all, he probably won't admit it.

Your feelings of embarrassment are normal. Eventually you'll find your way past it, when you're good and ready (and not before!).

NONVIRGINS: DID IT HURT THE FIRST TIME?
Oh yeah: 34%
A little: 40%
Nope: 26%

the human mind to have imagined that virginity could be

8

Yeah, the first time can be nerve-racking—especially if you're not quite sure what to expect.

No matter what else you've done with your BF, there's no telling what having sex with him is going to be like—if it's going to hurt, if you're going to bleed, if you're even going to like it. The thing is, sex is really different for everyone, and the only way to know what it's going to be like is to, well, actually do it.

Not that I'm saying that's what you should do.

Because the thing is, if you are that embarrassed about having sex, then maybe you shouldn't have it. At least not right now. I say wait until you're confident about doing it. And of course, when you do decide that you're ready, make sure you're protected.

If you feel uncomfortable just thinking about it, then you should give the situation some time and see how you feel about it later. —Tamar

I bet everyone on the planet has felt that way before. —krisna

i had sex. now i
feel used

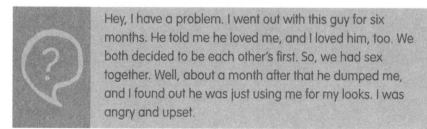

Hey, I have a problem. I went out with this guy for six months. He told me he loved me, and I loved him, too. We both decided to be each other's first. So, we had sex together. Well, about a month after that he dumped me, and I found out he was just using me for my looks. I was angry and upset.

a virtue.—Voltaire You're licking your lips and blowing kisses my way.

Then I started talking to this guy who is three years older than me. Well, one thing led to another, and we ended up sleeping together. After that he never called me again. Now I feel used and lonely.

The whole school knows about it, and my ex-boyfriend wants nothing to do with me. What should I do? Help me, please. How do I deal with this?

—DAYDREAMER

Tucker says

HEY, DAYDREAMER,

Okay, first: It's over, done. No matter how much you want to, you can't change the facts.

Next, give yourself a major talking to: Remind yourself that these experiences aren't who you are. They're over; you're still here. Make yourself promise you'll screw your head on straight when making decisions about sex in the future.

Next, point out to yourself that the gossip about you will pass with time, and other people's dirty laundry will eclipse yours. (I mean, that piece of news about me and the assistant principal blew over in no time flat.)

And finally, you may just have to suck up the fact that your ex doesn't want to hang. But dude, you said he was using you, anyway, so why do you still want to be with him? Give yourself a break. Cool?

fiona says

I totally agree with Tucker on this one. You can't change what happened in the past, but you do have the power to determine your future. At least in terms of what you do sexually.

But that don't mean I'm gonna give it away.—Christina Aguilera Like a

And if you know that you feel bummed and used and completely crappy when a guy blows you off after sex, you need to do your best to make sure that doesn't happen again.

The sad fact of the matter is that guys can say lots of stuff they don't mean to get you to give it up. Don't fall for it—be smart! So the next time you think you want to sleep with someone, don't just do it. Think about it, and wait until you're 100 percent sure that you're ready (and safe)—and that he's really worth it.

You need to stop going all the way just because they tell you they love you. —Cecelia

Virgins don't understand how much it hurts afterward when you feel used. —monielove

how can i tell if she's
really a virgin?

I am with this girl, and we've been together now for about two months. She says she loves me and that she thinks she's ready for sex.

But I want to save my virginity for another virgin. How can I tell if she's a virgin? I have asked her, but how do I know she's telling the truth?   —CONFUSED

virgin, touched for the very first time.—Madonna  Dolphins and human

tucker says

DEAR CONFUSED,

You can't know for sure.

But see, that's the thing. Deciding to have sex with someone means putting a lot of trust in them. When you do it, you're literally putting your body in their hands (not to mention other, uh, really personal places).

So before you go ahead and do the deed, you need to think about it. A lot.

And if saving your virginity for another virgin is that important to you, then you should make sure that you do that. For your own peace of mind. So you should have no doubt that the person you're about to give it up to is being honest with you about her sexual history.

And if it means that much to you, then maybe you should consider waiting to have sex.

fiona says

Yes, you gotta trust someone to sleep with 'em.

It's true, but still . . . What's this about requiring this girl to be a virgin? Like, I get the whole romantic notion of having that first experience together and being certain you've got all your STD bases covered, and there's probably some great moral thing in there and everything, but if you fall in love, you fall in love.

It's not fair to put that kind of limit on your love life. Take this girl, for example. What if you do fall in love with her, or decide you want to be with her, or realize you want to spend the rest of your life with her? Would you not let it happen because

> **WHAT DO YOU DEFINE AS HAVING SEX?:**
> Intercourse: 86%
> Oral: 47%
> Hand jobs/fingers: 15%
> Making out: 8%

are the only known animals that have sex for pleasure. Gazing at the

she's not a virgin? That doesn't seem fair . . . does it? I mean, how was she supposed to know she had to wait for you? Her virginity, or lack of it, says nothing about you. It's hers, not yours. There's way more to her than that, I promise.

If you luv her, you should trust her.
She says she's a virgin, then she's a virgin. —luvver

Why does it matter if your first is a virgin or not?? Are you afraid of looking bad? —heartbreaker

i'm 19 and still a **virgin**

I'm 19, and I haven't had sex yet. It's not really a choice or anything—I just haven't found the right guy.
What I'm worried about is that guys will be scared off when they find out. I know I shouldn't lie and say that I'm not a virgin, but what else can I do?
Thanks.

—VIRGIN BY DEFAULT

HEY, V.B.D.,

Repeat after me, "I am not a freak just because I haven't done it yet."

Excellent. Now say it again, just for good measure.

But seriously, being a 19-year-old virgin isn't that big a deal. According to a recent study by the Kaiser Family Foundation, 34 percent of graduating high school seniors are still virgins. That's a little more than one-third. And who knows if those people who did lose their virginity in high school were emotionally ready for it? Who knows what percentage of them had a positive experience? The bottom line is that you're your own person and you have to decide what's right for you. If you ask me, it's pretty smart to hold out for the right partner, and I think you should continue to do so. I mean, you've waited this long already, right? Don't turn something this important into a game of beat the clock.

And trust me, when you find the right guy, he won't be scared off by your virginity.

Hang in there.

tucker says

Scared off? Please, can you give us guys a little more credit than that? Most of us would be supportive—I mean, we have first times, too, you know? And how honored will the right guy be when he finds out you've chosen him?

Plus you gotta question a guy who'd freak about your virginity. If he has issues, he's not the right guy.

Hang on to your virginity until you're ready to do something with it. And don't make it an even bigger issue by lying about it to a guy.

Happy celibacy.

Not everyone in the world is screwing around, despite what they want you to believe. —BigV

Listen, if some guy threatens to dump you because you haven't done it yet, then you should drop him first. —Gungadin

of Souls 👥 I never miss a chance to have sex or appear on

virgin talk

I lost my virginity to a friend. We talked about it a lot before we actually did it. He was 19 at the time, and I was 17. My parents practically had a heart attack. Soon after, he went away (not by choice), and we swore to each other that we'd never break up and be together for life. . . . But times change and so do people.
—DINA

Hey, here's my story. My first time was with someone I thought was a good friend. We had talked a lot about having sex before it happened because there was a strong physical attraction. Sadly, I was dumb enough to fall for the "friends-with-benefits" routine. Basically I allowed someone to use me for my body and trample my spirit for TWO MONTHS! —BEEN THERE

My first time? Well, I was 15, and I had been dating the guy for almost two months (I'd known him for just over a year). We decided to go up to my room to "look for a CD." I was, honestly, a little nervous, and we didn't use any birth control, which I realize was very stupid. My first time really sucked. To put it plainly, I couldn't tell if he was in or out! My first enjoyable time was recently, and I wish I had waited for this guy to be my first. —JACINTA

We planned it ahead of time, for my sixteenth birthday. A week or so ahead of time my boyfriend took me shopping, and he bought me a dress that I could wear out that night and lingerie for our evening together. Then the night of my birthday, he brought me flowers and jewelry. We went to a beautiful restaurant and had a nice, romantic dinner. Then we went to the nicest hotel in the area. He'd had it all set up already with candles and romantic music. We started out just kissing and it was like any other time when we were playing around. We spent an hour at least, just on foreplay. I was completely turned on and ready when it finally came time for us to make love. We used a condom, of course, and it didn't hurt at all. It wasn't the best sex ever, but it still was a wonderful feeling. Afterward we wrapped ourselves up in a blanket and went out on the balcony and looked at stars. —TANTRA1

i **wanna lose**

my virginity

I really wanna lose my virginity bad because I don't wanna be the only virgin in the world, which I probably will be!

I'm also afraid it'll hurt. Is there any way that I can make it more comfortable? Please help!

Also, is it true that when you do splits and stuff like that, your hymen can break without you knowing?

~So Anxious~

DEAR ~SO ANXIOUS~,

tucker says

Okay, whoa! Slow down! You aren't, and won't ever be, the only virgin in the world. And since when is your virginity on everyone else's schedule, anyway?

I know how you're feeling. . . . There was a time when I was the only virgin in the world. But here's what I learned: Your virginity is an incredibly individual thing—everyone else's status has nothing to do with you. So slow down. If your friends are buggin' you about it, just give 'em a sly smile and a wink. They'll fill in the details on their own.

Now, will it hurt? I don't know. But I can drop this bit of info: The first time often hurts for guys, too. Thanks to all that friction and whatnot, many a poor guy wakes up with a sore thing after the first time.

> **IF YOU AREN'T A VIRGIN, DO YOU WISH YOU WERE?**
> Yeah, losing it was a mistake: 24%
> Nah, I'm glad I'm past that: 76%

Oh, and according to all those female anatomy books I've read (all us guys do, and that's a fact), there are all kinds of ways your hymen can break without you knowing. But FYI, none of them have to do with your virginity. Virginity isn't about the state your body is in—it's about whether or not you've had sex. And that's all it's about.

Your virginity, your call.

Fiona says

Excuse me, but where's the fire? I mean, what's the big rush to lose your virginity?

Especially since part of you—a big part—is scared and doesn't know what to expect. Time to stop focusing on your virginity and start focusing on yourself.

Plus if you're overly anxious about your first time—whether it's because you're uncomfortable with the person you're with, you're not protected, or you're not sure it's the right time—it could hurt more than usual. Because if you're not relaxed, your muscles tighten up even more than usual and then . . . ouch!

I think you should figure out what you really want. Take your time. And be yourself, not who you think the world wants you to be.

A lot of people say they're doing it when they're actually not, just for attention, so people will think they're cool. —Lindy

Don't waste it. It's something you can't take back. —Noel

overs and consequently used to break the legs of their male captives.

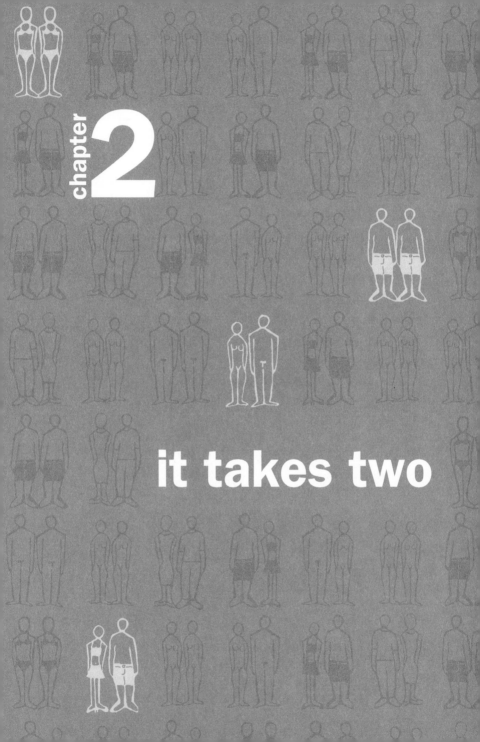

chapter **2**

it takes two

The best thing about sex is that it involves two people. And the worst thing about sex is that it involves two people. Not only that, it usually involves two people who are incredibly different from each other. (Hello! I'm a guy! And hello! You're a girl!) That's where it starts to get confusing. Which is why we're gonna talk about it in this chapter.

The thing is, if you're in any kind of relationship, chances are you and your partner are not on the same page on at least a few issues. Maybe your partner is ready to do more than you are. Maybe less. Maybe you're wondering how to say no, or yes, or whatever.

Just know that the most important thing you can do is communicate. Take the mystery out of things by asking questions. Not only because it will make you feel more confident about the decisions you make, but because, well, if you don't have the 411 on your partner, you're putting your body, and your mind, at risk.

See, you've got to put your own well-being first, and the way to do that is by getting the info you need. Then you can take into account how your actions are going to affect your health and your emotions and go from there.

So start talking—and listening—way before you start mashing. tucker

i feel guilty
about fooling around

Okay, I just broke up with this guy who was VERY experienced and pressured me a lot. I ended up going almost all the way with him. After he dumped me, I felt used.

Now I am dating another guy, and I really like him. He understands me, and although he is more experienced than me, he doesn't pressure me at all.

The only problem is, I feel bad about every little thing we do together afterward. Like before I would be fine with guys going up my shirt, but now even that makes me feel cheap.

It's so bad, I sometimes almost think that something is wrong with me. Why can't I just be like every other teenager? I mean, I'm not even tempted to fool around, yet I feel like I should, and I feel like I'm cheating my boyfriend out of what he should have.

—FRUSTRATED & CONFUSED

tucker says

DEAR FRUSTRATED & CONFUSED,

Okay, so I have no real idea why you feel the way you do about the stuff you do with the guy you're dating. It could be anything. From needing a break from guys in general to not being attracted to your current boyfriend.

She'll take a tumble on you. Roll you like you were dice.—Kim Carnes

But here's the deal: You shouldn't force it.

You aren't like every other teenager, F&C. You're you. And you just can't measure what you're doing based on what "every other teenager" is doing.

And you know what else? You aren't cheating your boyfriend out of anything because you don't owe him anything.

Except honesty.

I know you really like this new guy, but it sounds like being in a relationship might not be what you need right now. You've got stuff going on in your head that's keeping you from feeling comfortable with him. Not just on the fooling-around front, but on the being-together-and-trusting-each-other front.

I hate to suggest a breakup, but unless you take some time to focus on yourself, your new relationship isn't going to work out. I say take some time alone. He may understand this, and he may not, but what's important now is what's up in your own head.

> **HAVE YOU EVER BEEN PRESSURED TO HAVE SEX?**
> Yes, all the time: 13%
> Yes, once: 25%
> No way: 43%
> I'm not sure: 7%
> No answer: 12%

fiona says

Okay, your hang–ups may be putting some stress on your relationship with this new guy, but I dunno if a breakup is in order. It seems like you really like him and that you want to see where things go.

If that's the case, you should just tell this guy how you feel. That you've got some issues and kinda can't handle heavy-duty fooling around right now. That doesn't mean you guys can't still be together, right? If this guy is as cool as you say, he'll be able to deal without a little action for a while. Hooking up is something you do because you want to—not because you think it's expected or owed.

In the meantime, you need to really think about what your boundaries are sexually. What are you comfortable doing? How soon in a relationship do you want to get physical with someone? And what kind of level of commitment do you expect from a guy you're with?

Figure out that kind of stuff, and then apply it to your relationships. Don't cave because you feel like you have to do stuff to make a guy happy. Only do what you want to do, when you want to do it. That's the key. Stick to that, and I swear, you'll be feeling back to "normal" in no time.

Maybe you're not ready to start fooling around yet. —clavi

You aren't weird or anything—you just respect yourself, and that is so not a bad thing. —melinda

is he **using** me?

Last weekend I went to my crush's house to watch him play in his band. Afterward he started to flirt with me a lot. He told me that he had liked me for a really long time. We started to fool around, and he was being really sweet. He tried to push me to go further than I wanted to go, but I said no.

seafood, whole grains, and wheat germ. So get closer (closer now) to

But the fact is that he had a GF. He kept telling me and my best friend that he didn't like her anymore—and he was going to dump her, but he's still going out with her. And he's ignoring me at school. Since we hooked up, he's said about two words to me. I asked him to call me, but he hasn't yet.

So does he like me, or was he just using me? PLEASE HELP!

—VERY CONFUSED

DEAR VERY CONFUSED,

Not to be harsh or anything, but it sounds like he's just using you. Like he just wanted to see if he could get some action from you. And now that he realized you're not just gonna give it up, he's blowing you off.

It sucks, but it happens. A lot.

The truth is, some guys will say anything to get you to have sex with them. They'll tell you you're beautiful. They'll tell you they really like (or even love) you. The way to not get played is to use your head. Like you did.

There are a few ways to tell if a guy is just out for a piece. And band boy totally showed them all.

For starters, he's got a girlfriend. And although he told you he was going to break up with her—when he was trying to get some from you—he still hasn't. What's he waiting for?

And then there's the whole pushing-you-to-go-further issue. In my experience, guys who really like you don't do that. You were right not to let it go any further.

Sometimes I find myself wishing that girls would seriously call guys on that kinda stuff. I mean, saying, "But I'm going to break up with her," is the oldest line there is. Even I've used that one.

Lemme let you in on another secret: If you had given in, he probably would have blown you off, anyway, in the end. If you want to get respect from the fellas, you need to show them you're worth it by giving yourself some respect first.

Good luck.

You need a serious clue! He already has a girlfriend! —deb

You'll get over it—just keep telling yourself that he's a jerk.
—datruthruth

friends with benefits

Have you ever heard of the whole friends-with-benefits arrangement? Like a guy and a girl are friends and they hook up every once in a while, but they both know that they aren't going out officially with each other? Anyway, do you think it's a good idea?

—F.W.B.

DEAR F.W.B.,

Sure, why not? I mean, if both people are on the same page, and they're in full agreement, and everyone's being honest, I

During the mating season, deers' antlers become highly erogenous.

GUYS: WHAT'S THE WORST THING ABOUT GIRLS WHEN IT COMES TO SEX?
They expect you to know what to do all the time: 25%
They don't put out enough: 23%
They're teases: 22%
They get clingy: 13%
They're clueless: 7%
Other: 10%

think they should be able to do whatever they want.

But here's the problem: Too often, people settle for a "friends-with-benefits" arrangement when what they really want is something more than that. And when someone settles on that, it's only a matter of time before the whole arrangement goes sour.

You gotta be careful when getting into these situations, and you really do have to check your emotions at the door. If you can't do that—and most people really can't—then don't get involved.

It's not the best situation, but sometimes, well, it works.

GIRLS: WHAT'S THE WORST THING ABOUT GUYS WHEN IT COMES TO SEX?
It's all they think about: 28%
They expect you to look like a centerfold: 28%
They dis you afterward: 10%
They're selfish: 7%
They're clueless: 6%
Other: 21%

fiona says

Okay, I have to disagree with Tucker. I think that the whole "friends-with-benefits" gig is flat-out a really bad idea.

Here's why: When you're attracted to someone (even if that person is a friend) and you start becoming physical with them, it's supereasy to get caught up in the situation. And like it or not, you usually start confusing fooling around with something more.

You start out thinking that you can separate your feelings. Feelings that you'd normally have for someone who'd

What I got you gotta get it put it in you.—Red Hot Chili Peppers. Sex is want to spend time with you regardless of whether or not you're putting out. And then you begin wanting that kind of relationship—and becoming frustrated when you don't get it. Basically, friends with benefits is really hard to pull off. And a lot of times, I think it prevents you from getting a real relationship. Why waste your time pretending when you can have the real deal?

Right now, I am in
the same situation, and it's working out okay for me. —Amber

If I was you, I'd get a boyfriend and have a real relationship because having a friend with benefits can get very confusing.
—ramalama

i don't want sex to get
in the way

I've been seeing this girl for two years now—I've really enjoyed it, and we always have things we wanna talk about. Lately we've been talking about sex—including stuff like protection and all that.

We're comfortable and mature about it, but I just don't want to do it. I mean, I get aroused when I'm around her just by what she wears or how she says things or what perfume she has on. But still, I like the little romantic things we do. So I really wanna wait. I don't want a certain "thing" to get in the way. What should I do?   —KYLE

one of the nine reasons for reincarnation. The other eight are unimportant.

tucker says

DEAR KYLE,

Sounds like you have a tight relationship. That's cool.

Okay, here's the thing. There's no way you and your girlfriend will always be on the same page about everything. That's why communication is key. But you already knew that. After all, you two always have things to talk about.

But is there one little thing you aren't talking about? I mean, sure, you've got the 411 on protection and stuff like that, but have you really discussed having sex together?

Stop bugging, bro, and start talking. Who knows? She might want the same things you do.

And never, ever do it because you think you have to.

fiona says

You may not want sex to get in the way of your relationship, but it will unless you address it.

There's nothing wrong with a guy not wanting to have sex with his girlfriend—but if you start to avoid the topic, your GF may start to wonder if something's up—like, that you only like her as a friend or that you have some other issues.

So let her know how you feel and why you feel that way, right away. Just tell her, straight up, that you don't want to have sex—at least not right now—because you aren't ready for the complications.

She may not like it, but she should be able to understand it.

—Henry Miller Come on, baby, light my fire. Try to set the night on fire,

Hey, Kyle, I think you need to dump your GF and go out with me!!! You sound like such a sweetie! —deli

The best thing about it is that you two have already discussed it, so if it ever did happen, then you two would both be prepared. —punkin

how do i say no?

Hey, I have a question. My boyfriend is 16, and I'm 14. We have been dating for about a month and half, and I think he is going to ask me to have sex with him—but I feel uncomfortable 'cause I'm 14, you know.
So what do I say to him?

—NOT READY

DEAR NOT READY,

"No" works fine for me.

Seriously, if you know that you aren't ready to have sex—and to be perfectly honest, at 14 I think you're too young—the best answer is a simple, straightforward "no." That should get your point across to your BF. And if you're worried that being that direct might scare him off, preface it by telling him how much you like him and enjoy being with him, but that you're just not ready. But remember, your reasons are your own—you don't have to justify them to anyone.

If you don't feel like your boyfriend will accept your answer, then maybe you should think about if you really want to be with this guy in the first place. 'Cause having sex is a

yeah.—The Doors The oldest sex manuals were published in China

major decision—and it affects your life in serious ways. When you do the deed, you open yourself up to a lot of issues, including pregnancy, diseases, and seriously complicated emotions. Needless to say, it's a lot to deal with.

Your boyfriend is older than you, but he should still understand and respect that. And if he doesn't, then he's disrespecting you. Remember: You always have the right to say no. No matter how old you are, how long you've been together, whether or not you've done it before, etc.

Stick to your guns.

tucker says

There just ain't no way to say no except, "no." Believe me, I've tried.

And here's another reason. When girls say "yes" and they don't really mean it, guys pick up on that. And no matter what they tell you, guys don't like girls who say yes when they don't mean it. Sure, they'll stick around for some easy action, but in the long run, guys like girls who are confident enough to say what they mean.

Always put yourself first.

He is waaay too old for you. No wonder you can't talk to him. Get a new guy. —rondi

I am a guy and "no" is an acceptable answer, and if he doesn't accept it, it's called rape. —justin

,000 years ago. Sex is not the answer. Sex is the question. Yes is the

i can't get my boyfriend off

Okay, I've got this problem. It is, pretty simply, that I can't get my boyfriend off.

I've tried, but for some reason it's really bothering me that I can't—and lately I've been really down on myself for not being able to. At this point, I feel like I might as well not even try—so I end up just sort of teasing him.

I feel bad for doing that, but I know that if I try and it doesn't happen, I'll just end up feeling bad about it again. He swears that it doesn't matter to him, but I can't help but be bothered by it. What should I do?

—FRUSTRATED

DEAR FRUSTRATED,

If your boyfriend says it doesn't matter, then you have to believe him.

It's natural that you want to please him sexually, but there is more to getting it on than getting off. And if you only think about what you're doing with your BF as a means to an end—and you totally obsess about that the whole time—you're not relaxing and fully experiencing the moment.

Not to mention that you're also putting a lot of unnecessary pres-

GUYS: WHAT TURNS YOU ON MOST ABOUT GIRLS?
Body: 47%
Personality: 26%
Face: 11%
Brains: 3%
Reputation: 1%
Money: 2%
Other: 10%

answer.—Swami X. Damn, I wish I was your lover.—Sophie B.

sure on both of yourselves. Geesh, no wonder fooling around is so stressful for you. That, I'm sure, is a major part of the problem.

So my advice to you is to chill. Don't stop hooking up with your BF because you're afraid of not "performing" well enough. Every guy is different, and eventually you'll figure out how to make your boyfriend, uh, happy. Or you could always just ask him to give you some pointers. Whatever you do, be safe.

tucker says

There are lots of reasons why this is happening. Maybe your boyfriend's not quite comfortable with what y'all are doing, or maybe he's worried that he's not treating you well enough. (Believe it or not, lots of us worry about that.) Let him know that you're comfortable with all that you're doing (Are you? Check yourself . . .) and that you have a great time with him (Do you? Check yourself . . .). It should help to put him at ease.

And above all, trust him when he tells you not to worry about it. He really means it.

Don't tease him, just let him know how much you care for him.
—laura

Your guy says it doesn't matter, and that probably means he's in the relationship because he actually cares about you, so congrats on having such a great guy! —vane

Hawkins Sex appeal is 50% what you've got and 50% what people think

hollywood sex vs. real sex

Slow jams playing in the background, rose petals strewn across the bed, hot, passionate kisses—sex in movies and on TV is just about perfect. Too bad it's mostly fantasy. Just in case cable TV and Julia Roberts flicks were the main sources of your sex ed, here are a few reality checks:

HOLLYWOOD SEX: Sex is a mind-blowing, earth-shattering experience every time.

REAL SEX: Often one or both partners don't really climax. Sometimes all that moaning and heavy breathing means your partner is working up to a successful acting career, not an orgasm. (See: Deli scene in **When Harry Met Sally. . .**)

H: Doing it in exotic locations (an elevator, a bathroom stall, a car, the beach) is always hot and exciting.

R: Okay, (a) exotic usually means public, and if you get busted, you could get arrested. (b) Going at it in the Volkswagen isn't as easy or comfortable (hello, gearshift!) as it looks. (c) If you think getting sand in your bathing suit is uncomfortable, imagine getting it there.

H: Soft candlelight everywhere.

R: Hundreds of candles = major fire hazard. Plus you'll be scraping melted wax off everything for days.

H: Condoms? Who needs condoms?

R: You do, you do! Unprotected sex, meet your new friends STD and unplanned pregnancy. You'll be spending lots of time together.

H: Six-packs and perfect breasts.

R: The only real-life couple that looks like Tom Cruise and Nicole Kidman is Tom Cruise and Nicole Kidman. So stop stressing over those stretch marks, etc.

H: Choruses of, "Yes! Yes!" and plenty o' loud moaning.

R: Sometimes people make noises because they're enjoying the moment and want to convey that to their partner. But you're just as likely to hear, "Ow! You're pinching my arm," as, "Oh, baby! You're the best!"

H: Threesome? Sure, what the heck!

R: Threesome? Yeah, right! Chances are pretty slim you really know someone who's actually had one.

H: Food as foreplay: yum!

R: Marshmallow Fluff + body hair = ouch.

he hit me.
what did i do?

I was dating this guy for like a month, and he wanted me to have sex, but I told him no way. He asked me every day for like a week. When I told him no for the last time, he got really mad and hit me across the face, and he broke up with me.

So my question is, did I do the right thing, or should I have just done it?

—DAZED

fiona says

DEAR DAZED,

Yes, you did the right thing. It took a lot of guts to say "no" under pressure—but it was definitely the right decision.

You don't want to get involved in a sexual relationship with someone who is capable of being abusive to you. Physically or mentally. And this guy is obviously a total psycho &@*$! Oops, I can't say that here. But you catch my drift.

This guy obviously cares only for himself. Any guy who constantly pressures a girl to have sex doesn't really love her. He loves what he can get from her. You're worth more than that. Save it for someone who respects and cares for you.

I also think you should report the guy (to your parents or another adult you trust) so that it never happens again, but that's up to you. And if he does ever come after you again, call the cops.

you've got.—Sophia Loren In the movie *Pretty Woman*, Julia Roberts

tucker says

You so did the right thing. But let me just say that most guys aren't like that. It's guys like that who give the rest of us a bad name.

There is no reason for you, or any other girl, to stick with a guy who hurts you—physically, mentally, emotionally, whatever. There are plenty of guys out there who would never do that.

Stay away from him. Don't get suckered into dating him again. Too many times, girls forgive guys for stuff like this and go back for more. Don't do it.

Gimme his address—I'll slap him back! —Tatiana

He is total trash, and it's good that you set him straight. You go, girl! —franque

i said no to oral sex.
should he be mad?

Hey, there! All right . . . Last night my boyfriend asked me if I would give him oral sex. I said yes and didn't even think about it. . . . I have never done it before.

Well, we were getting pretty hot and heavy, and he kept trying to push my head down there. I was really scared to do it, so I just ended up giving him a hand job.

My question is . . . Was I really mean for telling him that I would give him head and not doing it? I feel horrible for doing that. As a guy (Tucker), would you be mad 4ever? Thanx!

—WORRIED GIRLFRIEND

had a body double for her sex scenes. Breathe out so I can breathe you in,

tucker says

DEAR WORRIED GIRLFRIEND,

Nah, I wouldn't be mad forever.

In fact, I probably would have gotten over it pretty quick. Come to think of it, most guys would have, too.

See, you're under no obligations here, no matter what you talked about beforehand. So it's not like you cheated him out of something he should have had.

Unfortunately, there are some guys, a few, who would get pissed off. That means you need to be careful. Because if you get the wrong guy in that situation, things could get ugly.

And while you definitely didn't owe him, you should still stay away from making any promises to anyone else about what you'll do before you're in a situation.

fiona says

You're not under contract here. What you decide to do sexually is entirely up to you. If you're scared or uncomfortable or just don't enjoy doing something, you don't have to do it. Ever.

And even if you say you'll try something, you have every right to change your mind.

So don't worry about it. If your BF is a good guy, he'll respect your feelings. And even if he is a disappointed he'll just have to deal.

One more thing: You gotta tell your BF to knock off the head-pushing thing. That's just gross.

If he gets pissed and dumps you, it's his loss. —kittenkaboodle

Quit worrying about him for a second and worry about yourself. —sam

hold you in.—Foo Fighters ⫯⫯ Before mating, earthworms produce a special

he threatened to
dump me

I need some help. My BF is 19, and I'm 16. Two nights ago we were IMing each other, and I asked him, "If I don't have sex with you, will you break up with me?" He told me if I didn't by his twentieth birthday, then he'd break up with me (his b-day is coming up). So I got really pissed off at him and wouldn't talk to him. Yesterday he came to see me at work, and I totally ignored him. Then last night, he e-mailed me saying that he was sorry, that he wouldn't break up with me if I didn't have sex with him, and that he hated himself for saying that in the first place.

I love him to death, but it really hurt me when he told me that. SHOULD I TAKE HIM BACK OR LEAVE HIM?

—DESPERATELY NEEDS HELP

fiona says

DEAR DESPERATELY,

I hope your jerk alert is going off, big time! It's so not cool for your boyfriend to give you an ultimatum about sex. Sex is a really big deal. And your BF should get that. (I'm guessing that's why you're pissed.)

But at least he apologized. Which means he realizes what an idiot he was. I'd let him grovel a bit more and then forgive him. Extreme randiness isn't grounds for dumping. But insensitivity is. So if your BF keeps pressuring you about doing the deed—and you're not ready—think about giving him the boot.

mucus to glue themselves together. If I put my fingers here, and if I say,

And if you do decide you're ready, you two should have a serious talk about it first—and make sure you're both ready with protection, too.

Peace.

tucker says

Okay, yeah, he said the wrong thing.

But he apologized and all. Give him a break. He's going out of his way to make things better.

And listen. What kind of question was that to ask in the first place? I think it's so uncool when girls ask questions like that, like they're testing us guys or something. It's like if we don't give them the answer they want, they're going to get all mad and make us grovel. It's a game, and I, for one, am not playing. And I certainly ain't groveling.

Be honest—don't be manipulative. And be careful what you ask . . .

> **GIRLS: WHAT'S THE SCARIEST THING ABOUT SEX?**
> Getting pregnant: 39%
> Getting an STD: 12%
> Whether or not I'm good at it: 10%
> Being known as a slut: 6%
> Pain: 5%
> That he'll be grossed out: 5%
> Getting dissed afterward: 5%
> Other: 18%

Hang on to him. I mean, who can resist a guy who can admit he's wrong?? —Neelie

Dump the chump. —chumpdumper

he told everyone we **did it**

I've been talking to this guy since March, and we go out a lot. Then a couple of weeks ago, I went to his house to watch a movie. Things got intense, and we ended up having sex. I was a virgin, and I didn't tell anyone, not even my best friend. That was Thursday, and that Sunday, a bunch of my guy friends knew about it. The guy swears he didn't tell and that one guy read his journal and spread it around. What do you think happened??

—WONDERING

tucker says

HEY, WONDERING,

Uh, you've been played. Sorry.

Now, I could be totally wrong, but there's something fishy about this tale of a journal and a nosy friend.

Why? (a) Because guys are even more secretive about their journals than girls are (if you can believe that), and guys keep that stuff hidden extremely well. If they have one (and that's a BIG if, at least among all the guys I know), their best friends don't even know about it and never will.

(b) If his friend read his journal, they

> **GUYS: WHAT'S THE SCARIEST THING ABOUT SEX?**
> Getting her pregnant: 31%
> Finishing too fast: 18%
> Whether or not I'm good at it: 16%
> Size: 10%
> Getting an STD: 9%
> Getting a bad reputation: 2%
> Getting dissed afterward: 3%
> Other: 11%

wouldn't be friends anymore.

(c) Not to generalize on gender lines or anything (but I will): Guys seem to be way more likely to boast about their sex lives than girls, at least when they're teenagers. (As people get older, that seems to switch. I mean, ever watch *Sex and the City*?)

I say he blabbed. Don't let him get away with it. . . . Make him admit it and apologize. If he doesn't, send him away. He's bad news.

As for losing your virginity, I think you should talk to someone about it, someone you can really trust—like your best friend. It's a major thing.

Peace.

Ideally, people's sex lives should be their own, and not grist for the rumor mill. If this dude told everyone, you have a right to be pissed. On the other hand, if he told only one person, I'd try not to be so mad at him. After all, having sex can be exciting, and people want to tell their buds about it. I mean, you'd want to talk to a friend about it, wouldn't you?

So talk to him, and find out what the deal is. He should apologize to you either way, but if he was bragging about his "conquest" all over town, then get rid of him. If he accidentally let the cat outta the bag, then cut him some slack. But if you do stick with this dude, make sure he knows that you want him to keep what you two do between the two of you.

I think that this guy just wanted to get player points for taking someone's virginity. He sucks. —Marla

Of course he told his friends! That's what guys do! Clue in! —babee

we only do it **when we're drunk**

I've been going out with an awesome girl for four months now. The problem is, we have sex like once a week or so, but we never do it unless we're drunk. I don't know why, but it's like we never really go there unless we've been partying or whatever.

I'd really like to hook up with her sometime when we're not drunk. What's the deal?

—JARED

DEAR JARED,

You shouldn't have to be wasted to be able to have sex with your girlfriend. In fact, doing the deed when you're sloppy drunk is generally a bad idea. It increases the probability of you two having unprotected sex (since alcohol can impair your good judgment) or having a condom mishap (since alcohol can impair your senses).

But it also says to me that you guys just can't deal with having sex when you're sober, and you have to dodge the issue by getting sauced up first.

So what do you do? Talk with your girlfriend. It's obvious that you're into each other, so tell her that you want to be with her when you're both sober. Try to figure out why you two aren't comfortable being intimate unless you're messed up.

And then decide if you are *really* ready to be having sex right now.

You come crash into me. And I come into you.—Dave Matthews

tucker says

It's called sex under the influence (SUI), and you and your GF are guilty! Okay, maybe it's not called that, but it should be. In fact, maybe we should start PADS (People Against Drunk Sex) and distribute brochures.

Whatever. Anyway, a lot of times I think people get into a rut about this. Like, the first time they hook up, they're drunk or whatever . . . then the second time, it's the same deal, and before you know it, you've got some kind of routine going— getting messed up, having sex, not talking about it, then not hooking up again till you've had another drink, etc., etc.

The good news is, you've identified the rut you're in. Now, sit her down and fix it. Before you get even deeper.

Oh, and to add fuel to your fix-it fire, there's the added issue of erectile dysfunction (you know, that special, uh, limpness), which happens way more often when you're under the influence. And Fiona's right: You are way, way more likely to end up a father, or a father with an STD or two, when you do it drunk.

Besides, since alcohol dulls your senses (and your orgasms), you're missing out on a lot.

Dude, that sounds like a bad soap opera. —alberto

My BF and I had the same problem. But we got past it and things are WAY BETTER now if you know what I mean.
—amandaG

When authorities warn you of the sinfulness of sex, there is an important

is he **too old** for me?

I'm 14, and my boyfriend is 18. He's a senior, and I'm a freshman. We've been dating for a couple of months, and we've started talking about having sex.

We aren't in a rush, but we've discussed using protection—both for STDs and preventing pregnancy. Basically, we've got everything in check should we decide to go through with it.

My only question is this: Is he too old for me? I mean, my dad keeps joking that my BF and I better not have sex— or else he'll have him thrown in jail. What's up with that?

—ASHLEY

HEY, ASHLEY,

Is he too old for you? Hmmm, well, in the law's eyes, that all depends on which state you live in.

See, every state has some kind of statutory rape law on its books. By this, I mean a law that sets an age (usually between 16 and 18 years) below which teens cannot legally consent to having sex.

So even if you agree to do the nasty with someone, if that person is over 18 (or in some states, even if they are more than a certain number of years older than you), they can be charged with having sex with a minor—and potentially go to jail because of it.

It seems a little weird that such laws exist, right? Well, originally statutory rape laws were created to protect minors from getting into abusive relationships with adults and to

esson to be learned. Do not have sex with the authorities.—Matt Groening keep teen pregnancy rates down.

The effectiveness of these laws is still subject to debate—and how they are enforced from state to state varies, as do those minimum ages. The best way to find out what the deal is in your state is to call your local Planned Parenthood at (800) 230-PLAN.

But when you're thinking about whether or not to have sex with your boyfriend, I say it's more important to consider your own readiness and maturity than statutory rape laws.

Yeah, your dad probably could make things tough on this guy if he wanted to. It wouldn't be the first time that's happened, either. Why? Because generally dads aren't all that into their daughters having sex with much older guys (or with any guys, for that matter).

And frankly, legal facts aside, he does have a point. I mean, not that your boyfriend necessarily has bad intentions or anything, but most senior guys hooking up with freshman girls don't have the best intentions in mind. He's probably got lots more experience than you with this stuff, and you've only been dating for two months. Know what I'm saying?

Think about it. . . . If you were a dad, wouldn't you be concerned? And besides, aren't you glad he's worrying about you instead of just blowing it off?

Statutory rape laws, and dads, aren't just there to get in the way of your life. They're there to help you out.

Do you two really love each other? If you do, it can wait until you are of legal age. —Arabica

I think that if you're in love enough and he respects you and you respect him, it shouldn't matter. —Daniela

Outstretched hands and one-night stands, still I can't find love.—Kid Rock

is cybering **cheating?**

My friends and I are having a big debate: If you are in a relationship and you cyber with someone else, is that considered cheating?
Confused,

—MANDY + FRIENDS

tucker says

HEY, MANDY + FRIENDS,

It probably is considered cheating by many people. They'd probably say that if you're in a committed relationship, you shouldn't be talking dirty with other people.

But I don't really agree.

To me, cybering isn't all that different from fantasizing and masturbating. It's just that you use the Internet for inspiration instead of whatever else you'd be using (a *Playboy*, a pic of Carson Daly, whatever floats your boat). You aren't hanging with anyone live, you aren't touching anyone else, you aren't, you know . . .

Still, I see why it's fuzzy . . . because on the other end of the connection there IS another person. But from what I can tell, no one who's out there cybering is really being themselves when they do it, so it's all fake, and that "person" you're cybering with doesn't really exist. See what I mean?

So my vote is no.

The exception: If you begin developing a relationship with someone on-line, even if it's cyber only, and if that relationship takes up a lot of your time and energy, then I'd say you may be crossing over into "cheating" territory.

Actual amount of semen per ejaculation: 1–2 teaspoons

fiona says

I agree with Tucker. Cybering with random people isn't cheating because there's no intent to do anything with 'em. There's no real connection.

But yes, some people would still feel threatened if their significant others were doin' the make-believe deed with someone else over the Net. The same way some girls get mad if their boyfriends read a lot of dirty mags or watch pornos all the time.

However, like Tucker, I would agree that if you're establishing an Internet relationship with someone (e-mailing all the time, cybering, making plans to meet, the whole shebang) — and you already have a boyfriend—then that's cheating.

I think it's cheating. Cybering can lead to a real relationship. —kane

If I want to cyber on my own time, and no one knows about it, then it's my business, and only my business.

Average number of times a man will ejaculate in his lifetime: 7,200

overage-underage?

Is it okay for an 18-year-old to go out with, and have sex with, someone under 18?

I DON'T THINK IT IS WRONG AT ALL!! I think if they really like each other, then it's fine! I'm 15 and I really like this guy, and if we went out until I was 17, he would be 19 then, and I would definitely have sex with him! **—ohio**

It all depends on the situation. If it's forced, then no. If they are both willing and are both protected, then yes. **—kitkat**

My boyfriend and I are willing to wait to do something in seven months, when I'm 18. If the love is true, he will be willing to wait for you until you're legal. **—jazmin**

18 and 17 is probably okay, but if an 18-year-old has sex with a 14- or 13-year-old, that's not—because the older one would be taking advantage of the younger one. **—damien**

sex and your social life

People love to talk about sex. Especially who is (or isn't) having it. I mean, why else would everyone be so obsessed with Madonna, Li'l Kim, and Pamela Lee? Basically because they've made careers out of putting their sex lives on display (either intentionally or unintentionally)—and the rest of us live out our sexual curiosities, fantasies, and anxieties through them.

It's no different in high school.

No matter what you're doing (or not doing) sexually, if people know about it, they're going to talk about it. And they're probably going to feel entitled to form opinions about it.

So for the next few pages we're gonna talk about what sex means to your social life—your friendships, your reputation, your social circle. Because like it or not, your decisions about sex are going to affect these relationships in a major way.

But whatever happens, and whatever you choose to do, just remember that your sex life is your own. And as much as people may try, they really can't judge you by what you do or don't do behind closed doors—or in the backseat of your car or wherever.

The only person's opinion that truly matters is your own.

fiona

players VS. sluts

Okay, what are your opinions on this? I don't get how when a chick messes up and screws some big-headed jerk one time (especially when she is drunk and too stupid to think straight), she is considered a slut by everyone—but when a guy goes and sleeps with any female he can get his hands on, he's cool. That really pisses me off.

—FIREBALL

DEAR FIREBALL,

It's a straight-up double standard. It's totally unfair. It sucks.

But luckily, not everyone thinks that way. Personally, I think a guy who sleeps around is equally as nasty, or maybe even nastier, than an easy girl. Why? Well, not only is he likely to be a big player and a liar (How else would he get so many chicks to give it up?) —but he's also a big loser. I mean, why else would he have such a low level of self-respect that he's willing to get it on with anyone who has a pulse? With all the risks involved in sex, that's kinda weak, you know? And even though it's not like people should be judged on their sex lives, why should anyone be commended for sleeping around?

Well, anyway, that's my take on the whole thing.

tucker says

Why is it like this? Why do guys get away with sleeping around? Well, because we can, and because everyone lets us.

Sad, but true.

And unlike Fiona, I don't think all guys who sleep around are total losers—many of them are just playing roles they think they're supposed to play. Just like girls who end up matching their "slutty" reputations because they think that's the best way to fit in.

Anyway, the slut-vs-player thing is a total double standard, and it's not cool, but it's up to people like you to change it. See, we can all sit around complaining about the way things are, but unless we do something about it, things will stay the same. That means defending people tagged as sluts, even if you don't like 'em . . . and challenging people tagged as players, even if you do like 'em. Until the Fireballs of the world actually start acting on this—taking down the "players" and lifting up the "sluts," then we're all stuck with the status quo.

I'm psyched you brought it up. Now, start bringing it up closer to home.

I hate that double standard. I say it is up to the girl what she wants to do with her body. And it is up to her if she wants to listen to what other people say. —Kittyboom

I have friends who could be considered players—and because of that, I'm sometimes ashamed to be friends with them. —Gfunk

what makes a player?

Seems like everyone has a different definition of a player. We always thought it was just a guy who fools around with a lot of girls, but . . . well, to a lot of people it's not quite that clear-cut after all. Check these:

A player plays around a lot, simple as that. —**DocPlaya**

I don't think sleeping with different girls makes you a player. A player is just someone who lies to girls. You could be a virgin and still be a player if you go around disrespecting girls. —**seleta**

Being a player means not being tied down by some clingy girl every time you want some. —**Ddawg**

If you hang out with players, people are gonna think you're a player. How are people supposed to see what you are like if they can't tell by the people you choose to hang out with? —**skitchit**

It's not just guys who play. I'm known as a player at my school, except I'm a girl and I play guys. Everyone knows I'm in control, so I'm a player, not a hoochie. —**Veronica**

Every player I know is just a poser deep down. The guys who are really getting laid are the ones who aren't bragging and talking about it all the time. Believe me, girls, the one you think is getting the least is probably getting the most. —**JasperJ**

should we have a
foursome?

My girlfriend and I have been going out for almost two years and having sex for almost a year. Lately we've been spending a lot of time with one of my good friends and his GF, who is also kind of friends with my GF. The four of us go out to eat and to shows and other stuff together.

The other night, after a party we all went to, my friend's girlfriend told me that she's in love with my friend, but she's been really attracted to me for a long time, too. And then the other day, my friend told me that he and his GF want to have a foursome with my GF and me.

I have to admit, I'm kind of intrigued by the whole idea, but I want your opinion. Is it wrong for all of us to have sex together? And what will happen to our friendship if we decide to go through with it?

—D.T.

tucker says

DEAR D.T.,

Is it wrong? Hmmm. Not for me to say. In fact, it's not for anyone to say.

Is it wrong for you? That's a different question. Again, it's not for me to say. Only you can make that call.

But I can tell you this: Couples that go through a group sex experience almost always run into problems. Problems with jealousy, boundaries, self-esteem, trust, and all kinds of serious stuff. You're walking on very thin ice. Some couples can deal with this stuff, but most can't.

Have you ever:
. . . had a three way?: 9%
. . . had group sex?: 6%
. . . played a sex-related game with your friends?: 31%
. . . had sex while drunk?: 24%
. . . had sex while high on drugs?: 14%

Before you even really consider it, you need to have a serious heart-to-heart with your girlfriend about it. Whatever you decide to do, it's incredibly important that you two stay on the same page.

And if you think safety is important one-on-one, it's even more so with multiple partners. Why? Because your chances of being exposed to an STD, even HIV, go way up. Think about it: You're doing it with three people, and those three people did it with more people, and all those people did it with even more people—and it all finds its way back to you.

Recently in Conyers, Georgia (an upper-middle-class suburb of Atlanta), dozens of teens tested positive for syphilis—all because there was a trend there to have group sex, play sex games, and stuff like that. The infection spread way faster than anyone could have imagined, and it seriously ruined many, many lives.

Although the idea of group sex might be intriguing, beware. It may be asking for trouble. Think hard before opening this can of worms and dumping it all over your relationship.

L8er.

Okay, here's my take on the whole group sex thing: It may work in the movies, but it doesn't fly in real life. Not if you have actual feelings for the person you're having sex with. Which, I assume, is the case with you and your GF.

See, if you're in love with someone, usually you don't want anyone else to be with them. In fact, the thought of it would be enough to drive you insane. Even if you agreed to it in the first place.

I'm not saying it's wrong—'cause who am I to judge—but I know people who've done it, and it's never worked out. It has always raised issues of mistrust, jealousy, and insecurity.

So before you do anything, think about it. Consider how it would affect your feelings about your girlfriend, your friend, his girlfriend, and yourself. Would it screw up your friendships? Make you feel like your girlfriend wants you less? Make your GF jealous of your friend's girlfriend? What would happen if one of the girls got pregnant? Think.

And if you do decide to go through with it, do only what you're comfortable with doing and be really, really careful.

EWWWWWWW!!!!! What will happen if this gets around your school? And what if your parents find out? —krissy

My friends and I decided to have one, but we put it off at the last minute. It's too weird seeing your BF with your friend.
Trust me. . . . —Jennifer

recorded: 11 inches Largest penis in the animal kingdom: 11 feet

i've got a **bad rep**

Can you please help me? Every time I go out with a guy, I end up having sex. Now I'm starting to get a bad rep with some of the girls in my school. What can I do?

—FREAKED

DEAR FREAKED,

Uh, for starters, you can quit having sex with every guy you go out with. Not just because it's bad for your reputation—it's bad for your health. Mental and physical. I mean, it sounds to me like you don't really want to be having sex with all these guys. So ask yourself why you're doing it. Do you feel you have to? Are you looking for love from these guys? Whatever the reason, it's time to take control.

> **IS YOUR REPUTATION IMPORTANT?**
> Oh yeah: 42%
> Kind of: 39%
> Not even: 11%
> No answer: 8%

Remember, you have a choice. You can choose to do it with every guy you go out with, but you can also choose not to. Next time try not to, and see what happens.

It sucks that your reputation is suffering, but enough is enough. You can prove that reputation wrong, and I suggest you do it.

fiona says

Having a slutty reputation seriously sucks, but you've got more important things to be worrying about. What about

STDs? Even if you use condoms, you aren't 100 percent protected from all types of STDs. And new research suggests that condoms may not be as effective in preventing the spread of the HIV virus as once thought.

Your health and your social standing aren't worth risking for people you don't even seem to really care about that much. So think before you give it up to every guy you go on a few dates with. Trust me, your rep—and your well-being—will benefit from it.

I think I know why you're having sex with all these guys. You want to feel liked, maybe even loved. You won't get it that way. —Alyce

What happened to actually dating the guy before you do the humpty dumpty?? —LauraMars

i'm worried
about my best friend

I'm really worried about my best friend. Today she told me that her boyfriend's best friend gave him a condom and told him to use it this weekend. So she and her BF are seriously thinking about having sex.

I keep encouraging her not to, and she keeps putting it off. But I'm afraid one of these times I won't be there to tell her not to do it, and she'll do it, and she might get pregnant! HELP!   —JENN

Distance sperm travels to fertilize an egg: 3–4 inches (The human

DEAR JENN,

Sounds like you're a great friend. Keeping an eye out for your girlfriend is a great thing to do. She's lucky to have you.

But she has to make her own decisions.

See, you can give her all the advice you want and encourage her to make smart moves and all the rest of it, but at the end of the day, you're not in charge of her life. As worried as you are about her safety and happiness, her choices are hers. Even when they aren't choices that you would make.

You two are best friends and all, so you should talk about this stuff as much as you want, but you have to let her decide for herself, and even if you think her decision is wrong, you've gotta stick by her. That's what best friends do.

fiona says

The bottom line is that your friend is going to do what she feels is right. Whether or not she decides to have sex with her boyfriend is a very personal choice. And I agree with Tucker—it's her choice, not yours. I hope you support her no matter what she decides.

It's obvious that your friend and her boyfriend are taking this decision very seriously and that they are going to be responsible about it. Don't worry. —Ella

It isn't even just her decision—it's their decision. —Robin

my friend won't **butt out** of my sex life

My best friend is driving me crazy! She thinks my BF and I should go further than we do. She doesn't get it that I wanna take it slow with him, and she tries to make us kiss all the time.

Help! I need serious advice.

—KAY

tucker says

DEAR KAY,

Okay, it's time for your friend to back off. Call her on the phone right now and tell her to chill out because it's none of her business.

There are all kinds of reasons why your friend could be acting this way. Like, maybe she's totally inexperienced and wants you to go through some stuff so she can get the low-down without doing it herself. Or maybe she's way more experienced than you and really wants you to catch up. Or maybe she's just crazy.

But no matter what her reasons are, she has no right to manipulate you into doing things you don't want to do. Tell her so, today.

What you do with your boyfriend is between you and him. How fast or how far you go is your decision. And nobody else's.

el 3–4 inches: 2.5 seconds. Time it takes an average person to complete a

So tell your friend to get her own life, her own boyfriend, whatever. And if she doesn't change, then maybe you need to hang out with your BF when she's not around, trying to force you guys to make out in front of her. 'Cause that's just weird.

My best friend pressured me to do a lot of stuff with my boyfriend and we went further than I wanted to. Now I'm known as a slut. —Alison

I think your friend is gettin' into your life 'cause she does not have one of her own!! —lazyeye

my friends are **freaking**
'cause i sleep around

 My friends are acting weird around me because I have sex with a lot of guys. What is their problem? It's my life.
—GEORGIA

tucker says

DEAR GEORGIA,

Your friends are acting weird around you because they care about you.

You're right. It's your life. It's your body. You get to choose to do whatever you want to do as long as you aren't hurting anyone.

But see, your friends think that you are hurting someone—

yourself. When you have lots of partners, you're more likely to get an STD, or get pregnant, or something like that. Plus sleeping around a lot can really get in the way of having a straight-up love-match relationship. Guys will start to see you as an easy lay, not girlfriend potential.

It is your life, and it is your body, and you are right to make your own decisions. But at least listen to other people's points of view—they have them because they love you.

fiona says

It is your life. But that doesn't mean you have to screw it up.

And like Tucker says, that's probably why your friends are freakin'. They want what's best for you—not a bad rep, a nasty case of crabs (or worse), or some seriously messed up emotions.

So try hearing your friends out.

If I were your friend, I would have yelled at you loud!! —Jacinta

I have no idea why they would act that way toward you, but I think that they are just jealous or something. —starbright

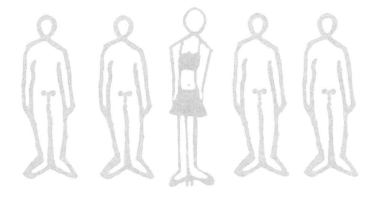

what they say, and what they really mean

GUY SPEAK

We're just friends.	I want to do it with her.
She's all right.	She's totally hot—she just hasn't agreed to go out with me yet.
She has a pretty face.	She's fat.
That dress looks really good on you.	Yes!! I can see your boobs!
Are you leaving already?	Does this mean we aren't going to get it on?
I don't care what we do tonight as long as we're together.	I don't care what we do tonight as long as it involves my tongue in your throat.
It'll be an expression of my love for you.	It'll be an expression of how horny I am.
Damn, girl, you're too hot to do it with a condom.	I don't wanna wear a condom.
It'll be just between you and me.	I'll tell all my boys. And every one else who happens to walk through the locker room.

Be it a compliment, a come-on, or just a little comment, you can't always trust that what members of the opposite sex say is what they actually mean. Here, a guide to help you crack the code.

GIRL SPEAK

We're just friends.	*I'd rather die a virgin than touch him.*
He's all right.	*Oh my God, he's so cute, I can't stand it! Do you think he noticed my haircut?*
He is such a sweetheart!	*I would never.*
Hey, where'd your friend go?	*If you don't get your cute friend back here right now, this conversation is over.*
So, what're you up to tonight?	*Ask me out now.*
I don't care what we do tonight as long as we're together.	*If you don't decide where we're going in the next ten seconds, I will kill you.*
I have my period!	*Stop touching me—it's not gonna happen.*
Let's just snuggle.	*Get your hand away from there.*
It'll be just between you and me.	*By tomorrow, it'll be like all my girlfriends have seen you naked.*

everyone thinks
i've had sex

Hey. My problem is that all my friends at school think I've had sex before, but the thing is, I haven't.

Well, now I'm afraid to go out with this girl because she might find out that I'm a virgin. But I really like this girl, and I don't know what to do. Telling the truth is not the answer, so please give me some other advice.

Thanks a lot,

—DESPERATE

DEAR DESPERATE,

Hey. Whether you've had sex or not is nobody's business but yours. So if you ask me, you don't have to say anything. Just make sure you're aware of what you want and be true to yourself.

It sounds like you're worried about going out with this girl. Don't be. There's nothing to be afraid of as long as you watch your back. If she really likes you, it won't matter if you're a virgin or not. I doubt she even cares. And if she does, she probably isn't the right girl for you.

The most important thing to remember is that you don't have to live up to your rep. In the end, the only thing that matters is how you feel—and trust me, you'll feel crappy if you aren't true to those feelings.

Be real. And just go with it.

to the penis: lavender, licorice, chocolate, doughnuts, pumpkin pie I

tucker says

Guess what? No one's reputation matches their reality, ever. No matter what you think you know about someone's sex life, it probably isn't true.

Now, about this girl—I think you're getting way ahead of yourself here. I mean, you aren't even going out with her yet and you're freaking about whether or not you're experienced enough for her! Time to check yourself and start taking one step at a time.

Being a virgin just shows that you have self-respect. If she can't understand that, then she's not worth your time. —Jenna

Don't start lying. It always backfires. —Delilah

his mother thinks
i'm a slut

I've been having this problem for a while now, and I would like to know if you could help me. I really love my ex-boyfriend. He's the love of my life and will always be. When we were going out, we—or at least he—didn't want to have to sex, so we got creative and just fooled around. And during one of those moments, his mother walked in.

After that, she made our relationship so bad, it got to the point that he broke up with me. Now everyone knows what happened and thinks I'm a slut. And I know he didn't tell. What do I do? Please help!

—CRISTY

believe in making the world safe for our children, but not our children's

HEY, CRISTY,

Having a bad rep sucks—especially when you did nothing to deserve it. People fool around with their boyfriends all the time. (Okay, so they don't get caught in the act by parents all the time, but it happens.) No need to make a federal case out of it.

If I were you, I'd try not to worry about the gossip too much. Someone (maybe one of your ex's friends) talked, and word got out. Whatever. There's nothing you can do now except damage control. My advice? Let it blow over. If you wanna talk about it with a close friend or two, that's cool—but you shouldn't try to defend your private life in public. That'll only make it worse.

So just chill, and all the behind-your-back talk will eventually die down. I swear.

tucker says

There's only one weapon against gossip: letting it die down.

While you're waiting, you might want to ask yourself if your ex is as perfect as you think. I mean, I know parental pressure can be a huge deal, but was it so bad that he had to break up with you? And if he didn't tell anyone about what happened between you guys in his bedroom, how does everyone know? Could be the guy is totally innocent, but maybe you should consider the possibility that he's not all that after all.

Later.

Welcome to Sexism 101. If everyone wasn't calling you a slut, they'd probably be saying you're frigid. —checkit

Don't sweat it. Next week there will be a new "slut." —bedazzle

children, because I don't think children should be having sex.— Jack

i'm **not a player—**
but she doesn't believe it

I'm known as a player at my school. I guess it's because some of my friends really are like that. They're always hooking up with girls, dissing them, hooking up with them again. . . . You know how it is. But I'm not like that. I've only done it with one person.

Last weekend I talked to this really cool girl, and I thought we connected, but she told her friend she wouldn't go out with me because she knows all I want is to hook up. Which isn't true. How am I going to get her to see I'm not a player?

—ALAN

tucker says

DEAR ALAN,

Damn, I hate that whole guilty-by-association thing. I get that a lot. Like, people think I'm a freak when I hang out with Fiona, but I'm really not.

Anyway, if you ask me, it's really unfair for this girl to judge you based on who your friends are. But, I guess it's understandable and all because we all make judgments like that.

Since you two "connected," there's still a chance for you. She obviously saw something in you that she likes. So if I were you, I'd figure out how to be in the same place at the same time as this girl again and talk to her about this.

Be aware, though, that the first thing a real player will say to a girl he wants to get with is, "But baby, I'm not a player." But I

68

think if you're straight-up honest, she'll believe you. And if she still refuses to see the real you, she's not worth your time.

Wow, being judged by who you hang with really sucks. But it happens. A lot. And when you think about it, it makes sense. I mean, most people gravitate toward people with common interests and values, right?

You just need to let this girl see that you're not like your friends. She might buy it . . . or not. It is quite possible that she won't be willing to take a chance on you.

And as wrong as that may be, it's a fact of life. 'Cause dudes like the ones you hang with give all guys a bad name. They make us girls distrustful and put us on the defensive.

If you're gonna hang out with the "player crew," then you have to realize that you're gonna be seen as one of the players. —nanya

My boyfriend is just like you and I also judged him by who he hung out with. So he started writing me letters and saying "hi" and not acting like a butt-head when he was around his friends. —Jenna

why do **hoochies**
get all the love ?

Are guys just interested in slutty girls? Because it seems that all the girls who wear hardly any clothes get more guys, and the rest of us (like me—I refuse to go around half naked to attract guys) never get guys. THANKS!

—KOLE

 Jennifer Lopez Sex on television can't hurt you unless you fall off.—bumper

tucker says

HEY, KOLE!

Okay, here's the deal. Yes, girls who go around half naked get more guys. That's because when most guys see skin, they want booty.

Sure, lots of guys may go for girls who flaunt what they've got, but those are the same guys who dump those girls as soon as the next piece o' booty strolls by. These guys are commonly known as players, and you don't really want to have anything to do with them, anyway. Besides, most players aren't players for life, and once they're done with being players, they lose all interest in the girls who wanted to get with them back in the day.

So unless your goal is to be a hoochie mama, you're doing all the right things. You're being yourself and refusing to play with the players. Good for you.

fiona says

I'm impressed. Sounds like you know that what you're worth as a person is not dependent on how many guys are checking you out—or even asking you out. You've probably got your mind on more important things than catching a guy's attention.

A guy who appreciates that will show up soon enough.

Do you actually want one of those guys who flock to the half-naked girls, anyway? Personally, I hate that type of girl. —Juan

Yes, hoochies get more guys. However, it's about QUALITY, not quantity, hon. . . . —lisa

sticker 👥 Ooo-eee baby, I'll sure show you a good time.—Steve Miller Band 👥

hoochies speak up!

I am willing to do things with guys. . . . I think of it more as fun and experimenting! I mean, I am a girl and I just wanna see what a guy is really made of! —**hyperchik**

ok, i guess you could say i'm a hoochie. well, actually i guess i just enjoy giving head. so yeah, that's me. i don't know why i do it, i just like to make guys happy. i only do it to guys who i KNOW would never hook up with me, but it's fun to get affection from them for a while, you know? i can't help it, i enjoy it. —**pellmell**

Yeah, I've slept with enough guys that I'm counting them on my toes now, but it's my life and my choice—just remember that in 2000 it requires safety. —**zcandal**

Well, I wouldn't say I'm a hoochie really. . . . But I have been known to have sex with random guys at parties and such. I was 16 when I lost my virginity, so I wasn't too young. And I'm trying to keep my numbers down. As much as I remember, I'm only at four or maybe five guys. I ALWAYS make sure they use a condom the entire time and use it properly. I do have a reputation at my school as being a slut, though, which is not cool. —**fleur**

yes, everyone at my school thinks i am a slut. i am not and i am sick of it. i never did anything with a boy in my whole life besides a lame little kiss! —**shauna**

prudes talk back!

Why am I a prude? For many reasons: I was a late bloomer, so I just wasn't interested very early on, I've always been very smart and known what it was that guys were trying to get, and I'm picky. All my friends lost their virginity in high school, but I'm in college and still a virgin. **—bana**

Yeah, I am pretty sure that some people may think that I am a prude. You know what, who cares? I at least don't want to get a BAD rep. If I have to have one, then it is better to be a prude than a hoochie. **—chicslick**

Okay, people definitely call me a prude. I am 14 and haven't even had my first kiss yet. I am still waiting for it to be special and for me to be ready enough—no one understands this but ME!! But oh, well, I don't care—I am waiting for the perfect time, person, and place. **—buttercup**

I would like to say that guys respect girls more when girls don't hooch out to them. Guys respect me and understand how great a girl can be without "givin' up the drawers." To all those girls who are hoochies, keep up the good work because you all are making more guys run to us.**—Stel**

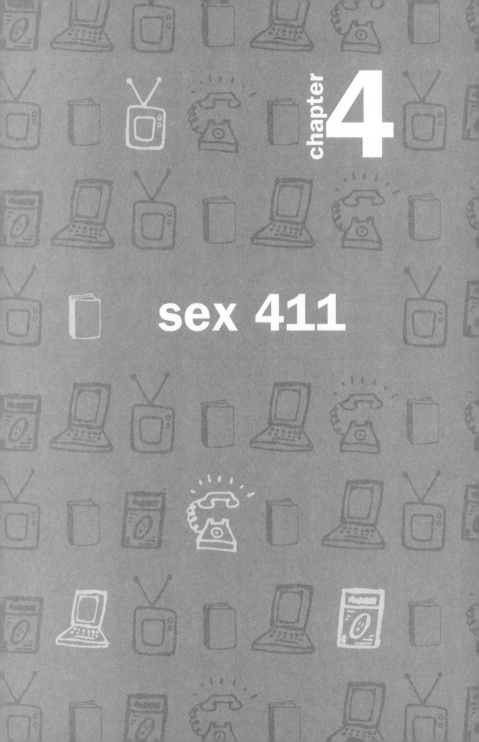

chapter **4**

sex 411

Since we all talk about sex so much, and since we see it all over the media, it makes sense that there are all kinds of rumors, ill information, and random terminology floating around out there.

And there's nothing more embarrassing than using the wrong word or having the wrong info, either while you're getting down or just hanging with friends. (Like just the other day, I used "the water method" —see page 85—in a sentence incorrectly. Fiona laughed at me so hard, she almost hyperventilated.)

This section is all about clearing up the confusion.

No snickering, please.

where &
where not to get your sex info

When it comes to sex, everyone's got something to say. So, how do ya know who to trust when it comes to dispensing nuggets of nookie wisdom? Check out our quick guide to getting trustworthy sex info.

POSI-SEX-FO
(the Quality Goods)

A TRUSTWORTHY ADULT. Yeah, we know the thought of trusting one of those dinosaurs with any of your sex issues makes you want to puke. Hold your gag reflex, and get a family friend or older cousin on the phone. They've been there and done that. Oh, and that, too.

A PEER COUNSELOR. Lots of schools and religious orgs have teen volunteers who are open to discussing your sex concerns. Talk to these peeps 'cause they're less intimidating to talk with than adults, plus they know what's up in the NOW.

THE LIBRARY OR BOOKSTORE. They have to be useful for something. At least you know this info's reliable. Start with the ultimate female sexuality power manual, *Our Bodies, Ourselves for the New Century*.

SEX-SAVVY SITES. Now that we live in a twenty-first-century robot world, the fastest way to get up-to-date info on anything, including sex, is on the Web. Of course, you're better off going to reliable sites like Alloy.com.

DOCTORS. First off, nothing can scare them. They played with cadavers in med school! Second, they have to keep everything you say on the hush-hush because of doctor-patient confidentiality laws. So, they're not gonna be calling your parents and asking if they know what you've been up to in the backseat.

PLANNED PARENTHOOD. It's confidential and free and employs people you can openly discuss the most embarrassing questions with. Nothing you say can possibly faze them. Plus, free pamphlets!

NEGATORY SEX-FO
(Argh! Run!)

ANYBODY WHO USES THE TERMS "BANGING BROADS," "KNOCKING BOOTS," OR "GETTING MY SWERVE ON." Shudder.

YOUR BEST FRIEND'S OLDER BROTHER. This is the guy who couldn't keep his eyebrow ring from spewing that totally icky infection. For all the talk Pus-head's been doing since you were in the second grade, what are the odds he's actually ever had sex?

SONG LYRICS. Though they may seem helpful at first, lyrics like, "You're a big fine woman when you back that thing up," and, "I did it all for the nookie," aren't as useful when you actually use them.

TALK RADIO. Don't listen to anything Howard Stern says, ever. Oh, and kissing a girl in a radio studio for prizes does not make you a lesbian.

TV. Real sex isn't all scented candles and blurry camera work. Sometimes it's overlit, slimy, and not too glamorous. And in TV land, consequences only have to be dealt with as long as they can be resolved in under an hour (a half hour, if we're talking prime time!). Don't believe the hype. (See page 32—Hollywood Sex vs. Real Sex.)

VIDEO GAMES. Especially ones about going to a bar and getting inhumanly shaped Amazon women to sleep with you. Or games about blowing lots of people's heads off, only to be rewarded with Amazon women. That just isn't how it works in life. And when was the last time you saw one of those Amazon women hanging around, anyway?

i have a small penis

After having heard all of the rumors about a normal penis size being about six to six and a half inches, I became really frightened because, well, mine isn't even five inches long.

I hear people talking about 14-year-old guys who are seven inches, and I'm 17. Am I going to be tiny forever??

—J.

tucker says

DEAR J.,

Listen up. There's way more to life than getting out a ruler and measuring your ding dong. It's a waste of time and energy.

Okay, that said, you might still grow some. Deal is, your business will probably keep "filling out" for a while—for most guys, right into their early twenties. So eat right and stay healthy, and who knows?

Oh, and news flash: You can't listen to gossip about size. It's never, ever true.

> **WHERE DO YOU GET YOUR SEX INFORMATION?**
> Friends: 61%
> Siblings: 2%
> Parents: 3%
> School: 7%
> Books: 7%
> On-line: 11%
> No answer: 9%

fiona says

Yeah, dude. Don't believe the hype. The average length of an erect penis is six inches, but the range is anywhere from about four to eight. Just like height and eye color, penis size is determined by genetics—so it's different for every guy.

Smallest natural penis recorded: $\frac{5}{8}$ of an inch Anyone who eats

And for the most part, girls expect and are cool with that.

Sure, there are a few size queens out there, who insist that having sex with a bigger guy is better. But really most girls would rather be with a cool guy than some jerk with a big package. So don't stress.

Besides, haven't you ever heard: It's not the size of the ship, but the motion of the ocean? That's no joke.

Look here . . . It doesn't matter how big or small your penis is. What really matters is what's on the inside (and I'm not talking in your pants). —Jancee

Unless you are some aspiring porn star, who is going to care? —Dawrya

what are **wet dreams?**

I'm a girl, and I always have sex dreams about boys. Are these wet dreams? And if not, what are wet dreams? I know guys get them, but can I get them? Thanks.

—STRAWBERRY

DEAR STRAWBERRY,

Well, technically, they aren't exactly the same as wet dreams. They're a little less, uh, sticky. But a sex dream is a sex dream is a sex dream, if you ask me. When a guy has a wet dream, he basically orgasms in his sleep. He may or may not manually go for it (sometimes that does happen!), but his dream is hot enough to produce an ejaculation.

When a girl has the equivalent of a wet dream, she also may or may not stimulate herself using her hands, but the dream still takes her there, sometimes producing an orgasm.

Oh, and both guys and girls also have plenty of sex dreams that don't go all the way, no orgasms.

Enjoy!

fiona says

Tucker pretty much dropped the science on that one, so I'm just gonna add that not all wet dreams are caused by a guy actually fantasizing about sex while he's asleep—at least not that they can remember.

Sometimes they come out of nowhere—they're basically a sign that a guy's body is producing sperm. That's why they usually begin to happen when a guy's around 12 or 13 years old. Wet dreams occur less frequently as a guy gets older and as he ejaculates more often when he's awake.

Peace.

I have never had one and I'm 16, but I'm sure it happens. —Amidana

I'm a girl and I have dreams about sex and boys alllll the time! It's great! —prepmax

three to one.—Marilyn Monroe Movies set up unreal expectations for

what does **69** mean?

What significance does the number 69 have?

—CONFUSED

DEAR CONFUSED,

Uh, I have no idea.

Okay, just kidding.

I remember running around screaming, "69!" thinking I was the coolest person on the planet, when really I had absolutely no idea what it meant. 69!!! Sixty-nine!!!!! Siiiiixty-niiiine!!!

My mother was like, "Okay, kid, you are really annoying."

Anyway, it refers to a sexual act. The one where both people are performing oral sex on each other at the same time. Picture it.

The thing that I don't understand is why people get such a charge out of saying it or using it in their screen names or whatever. It's just, like, okay, whatever. Sixty-nine. You're cool. No one's ever thought of THAT before. Know what I'm saying?

I always heard that the round parts of the six and the nine were supposed to represent the two people's heads. Does that help ya out?

C'mon, even I knew what 69 meant and what oral sex was when I was in like fourth grade! —Whateva

What's so cool about 69!! I just don't get it. —Radattack

how fabulous [sex] should be.—Cindy Crawford What a day, eh,

sexicon

Sex can be kind of funny and strange, right? Well, no wonder. Think of all the funny and strange names we use to describe it. Below, a list of sex terms that you'll never hear in health class but probably will in the locker room or back of the bus.

Beer goggles: An excuse for hooking up with someone you normally wouldn't. Commonly occurs during freshman year of college, thanks to the haze of too much booze.
As in: *I can't believe I hooked up with that ugly guy! Guess I was sportin' some beer goggles.*

Blow job: To give oral sex to a man. Also known as fellatio, going down on, giving head, sucking off.
As in: *We decided we aren't ready for sex yet, but I did give him a blow job.*

Blue balls: See "oldest trick in the book." Refers to testicle discomfort allegedly suffered by men as a result of being sexually aroused without release/ejaculation. Often used as a pressure tactic to talk women into having sex. Note: There's not a single case of "blue balls" that cannot be cured through masturbation. Next time your

partner complains about it, introduce him to his hand.
As in: *C'mon, baby. You don't want me to get blue balls, do you?*

Booty call: Late night get-together for no other purpose than to get a quick piece.
As in: *You two did not get together to watch* SNL *last night—that was a booty call.*

Born-again virgin: One who's technically lost his/her virginity but has either renounced sex or gone so long without it, he/she may consider him/herself a "virgin" again. (Note: Let them believe this even though it's bogus.)
As in: *After her last disastrous relationship, Beth said she was going to give up sex and become a born-again virgin.*

Dildo: Fake penis often made of rubber. Commonly used for—although not limited to—female masturbation and lesbian sex (for penetration). Note: Usually absurdly larger than the average real penis. Don't be fooled.
As in: *Dildos come in three sizes: large, extra large, and you wish.*

Doggy style: A sexual position that mimics the way dogs have intercourse (female on all fours with the male entering from behind).
As in: *Doggy style is a good sexual position if both parties want to watch the Discovery Channel while having sex.*

Drought: Slang for going long periods of time without sex. Similar to born-again virgin, although with a slightly more negative connotation since the celibacy is rarely by choice.
As in: *Man, when is this drought gonna end? I could really use some booty.*

Dry Sex: Simulating sex without actually having intercourse, while clothed or partially clothed (or naked, in some cases, as long as there is no penetration).
As in: *My boyfriend and I arent ready for sex yet, but we have had dry sex.*

Eat out: To give oral sex to a woman. Also known as box licking, cunnilingus, going down on, licking carpet, muff diving.
As in: *My brother is so immature that whenever my mom asks us if we want to eat out, he starts laughing.*

Feel up: Most commonly refers to going up a girl's shirt and fondling her breasts. Way back when, it was known as second base.
As in: *I can't believe that idiot tried to feel me up right in the middle of the movie!*

Finger: Inserting finger/fingers into the vagina and/or stimulating the clitoris for sexual pleasure.
As in: *Always remember to use antibacterial soap before fingering.*

Golden shower: Sexual fetish in which one person urinates on the other. Also called water sports. No diving board needed.
As in: *I don't even like cleaning the toilet, so what makes you think I'd enjoy a golden shower?*

Hand job: Using one's hand to stimulate the penis to cause orgasm. Also known as jerking off and getting off.
As in: *Whenever I see my brother head to his room with Lubriderm, I know it's hand job time.*

Jizz: Often used to describe both male and female sexual body fluids. Also known as gizz, gysm, cum/come, spoo, spooge (female only: juice, soup, gravy, nectar).
As in: *Dave, there's a spot on your pants. Wait, is that . . . jizz?*

Knocking boots: Intercourse; the actual sex act (the insertion of the penis into the vagina). Goes by many names, most commonly bumping, doing the nasty, home run, nookie, screwing, making love, humping, hiding the salami, going all the way.
As in: *If he refuses to wear a condom, there'll be no knocking boots on the evening agenda.*

Knocking on the back door: Anal sex. Also known as Greek style.
As in: *It's hard to believe that in many states knocking on the back door is actually illegal!*

Orgy: A sexual encounter involving more than three people.
As in: *Wow, there were four naked people in bed together. It must have been an orgy.*

Queef: Sound often made during sexual intercourse as a result of air pockets getting trapped in the vagina during thrusting of the penis. Basically sounds exactly like it's spelled and is almost always amusing when it happens.
As in: *I used to be embarrassed if I queefed during sex with my boyfriend, but now that we've been together for so long, I don't even let it bother me.*

Shrimping: Toe sucking. Despite the name, does not normally involve cocktail sauce or melted drawn butter—unless you're into that sort of thing.

As in: *He may be a shoe fetishist, but he thinks shrimping is totally gross.*

Swing both ways: Bisexual (sexually attracted to both males and females). Also known as playing for both teams and switch-hitting.
As in: *Although it's been said that David Bowie swings both ways, he denies that he was ever into men.*

Threesome: Sex involving three partners simultaneously.
As in: *For many heterosexual men, having a threesome with two women is the ultimate fantasy.*

Water method: (1) Masturbating while in the shower or tub, (2) using a water stream from a shower head to sexually stimulate a woman, (3) the cause of skyrocketing water utility bills in households with horny adolescents.

As in: *Just because I took a superlong bath doesn't mean I was doing the water method.*

Whacking it: To sexually pleasure oneself manually. Also known as beating off, getting off on yourself, giving yourself a hand, relaxing with your thoughts, self-love (female only: making soup; male only: choking the chicken, jerking off, spanking the monkey, wanking off).

As in: *I can't even eat apple pie now without thinking of that guy whacking it in* American Pie.

i think **i smell**

The other day I was with my boyfriend, and we were doing stuff, and I noticed that my southern area has a really strong smell to it. Is this normal? And is there anything I can do to help it?

—HEIDI

fiona says

DEAR HEIDI,

Are you sure it's a "strong" smell? Because, you know, it's perfectly normal to have a little odor down there. Both male and female sex organs have distinct smells and tastes. It's natural.

In fact, biologically speaking, those bodily scents are supposed to be a turn-on to the opposite sex. If anyone makes you feel otherwise, then maybe you shouldn't be hooking up with them.

The bottom line is that you should be comfortable enough with your own body not to feel self-conscious about a mild odor. 'Cause if you shower regularly, you should be all set. There's no need to do anything else. Even though commercials for those "feminine deodorant sprays" would have you believe otherwise. (Actually, you should avoid douching or using those sprays because they throw your body's chemistry outta whack.)

But if you really do notice a truly foul smell down south— or if you experience itching or irritation—then you could have a vaginal infection, and you should go to your gyno right away.

Yep, believe it or not, that scent is a full-on turn-on to most guys. In fact, biologically and evolutionarily speaking, that's exactly what it was designed for.

So you're on track with that.

But here's the thing: Are you sure you're ready to be "doing stuff" with your boyfriend if your "southern area" is still a mystery to you? I mean, if you ask me, you oughta really get to know your equipment first before you start putting it to use.

More comfortable reading than asking someone? Hit the library or bookstore for some legit info on the subject. (And see page 74—Where to Get/Where Not to Get Your Sex Info.)

And oh yeah, if your fella freaks about it, he also needs some schooling. In fact, he probably needs some schooling, anyway—most guys do. Guys—get a book, read up. You should know what's up down south, too.

It's natural to have some little odor, but anyway you should go to a gyno if you're sexually active. —Tantra

Is that really a turn-on to guys? I find that hard to believe. —dre

do guys only think about sex?

My friend recently told me that guys think about sex 24/7. Is this true, or is it just some guys and not others?

Sincerely,

—CONFUSED

ex with them—as is my understanding.—Bart Simpson Sex is

tucker says

DEAR CONFUSED,

No! (Sex) I have no (sex) idea what you're (sex) talking about (sex)! (Gee, I wonder if I'll get any tonight?)

Okay, fine. Guys think about sex a lot. But dude, so do girls. Maybe guys do talk about it more, and that's where this myth comes from. Or maybe it's because we live in a world where it's more "acceptable" for guys to think about sex than it is for girls. Who knows? The point is, we all think about sex, a lot. But we also make time to think about other stuff. You know, like school, Radiohead, the dog.

fiona says

Yes, both men and women think about sex. A lot.

But I think the idea that guys think about sex all the time is a myth, perpetuated by stuff in our culture like *The Howard Stern Show* and *Baywatch*. Why? 'Cause let's face it—sex sells.

But there is a limit. If people had sex, and only sex, on the brain all day long, not a whole lot would get done. So rest assured that there's a lot more going on in everyone's minds—that's true for guys as well as girls.

Believe it or not, some guys think about love, too. —Adam

I wish I was a guy so people would think it's cute when I think about sex all the time. —tanesh

DO YOU THINK ABOUT SEX TOO MUCH?
No, definitely not: 8%
There's no such thing as too much: 67%
Yeah, I'm obsessed: 25%

emotion in motion.—Mae West You talk like sex.—Dru Hill

does **hollywood** influence your **sex** life?

Kids should know what's right and wrong without the influence of movies. I mean, if some kid went and saw <u>American Pie</u>, would they go home and shove a flute up their . . . yeah. I don't think so! Not unless they were completely stupid or just REALLY WEIRD. —**dudetta**

Television, movies, and music all influence our lives! People think they're losers if they aren't doing it like everyone on TV. Think about it. —**randall**

I think parents today need to wake up and start doing their jobs. There has got to be a point where they stop letting everything and everyone else be in charge of us when it should be them. —**dariagrl**

it's like, embarrassing to go to the movies with ur friends and end up watching two big goons making out! violence i can deal with, but sex, come on! it's like, where has all the decency gone?! if u want to watch sex, go visit a porn theater. —**laurag**

protection and STDs

chapter 5

Y'all: Use condoms. I don't know how else to say it.

Actually, I almost feel like I shouldn't have to. I mean the whole "safe sex" message is all up in your face everywhere you look—on TV, at schools, in magazines, in books like this.

In fact, it's such a common message that it's easy to ignore. Don't. "Use a condom" is a cliché for a reason: because it's true. If you don't, you could die.

Death not a problem for you? Okay, try warts on your weenie. Open sores on your coochie pop. Blood in your urine. Searing pain when you pee. Shots. More shots. Shots where you don't want 'em. Lengthy discussions with your mom about why you're popping penicillin five times a day. Pus oozing out of places it shouldn't. Never being able to have children.

According to the World Health Organization, 3 million American teens are diagnosed with STDs each year. That's a lot of teens. And many, many more are never diagnosed, which means they could be spreading stuff, possibly in your direction.

Grossed out? Good, that's the idea. Because I guarantee you'll be 95,000 times more grossed out if you have to deal with this stuff live.

Bag it. Period.

tucker

most common STDs

STDs suck. Frankly, from AIDS to HPV, it's one big, icky subject, and we hate it. But pretending like it's not there won't make it go away: If you're having sex, you're at risk—period. You can protect yourself, though—and your partners—by educating yourself about STDs, making sure you're tested for them, and taking the steps (like using condoms or abstaining from sex) that'll keep you from ever getting them. Now, we're no scientists, so if you're wondering about any of these STDs, you should talk to a doctor or consult a book on the subject, but here are a few of the biggies we think you should watch out for:

Chlamydia

What it is: Microscopic parasite.

What it does: The parasite infects both men and women, down around the vagina, penis, urethra, cervix, and/or fallopian tubes. If untreated, it can cause lasting pain (especially when you pee), discharge, and even sterility in some people. Plus it increases the risk of contracting HIV.

How it's spread: Vaginal and anal intercourse and from a pregnant woman to her fetus.

Symptoms: Often none. Sometimes a burning during urination or vaginal or penile discharge. Women may also have pain in the lower belly, pain during sex, or bleeding between periods.

Treatment: Antibiotics. Both the infected person and that person's partner take either doxycycline or azithromycin. Doxycycline is less expensive but must be taken for seven days; azithromycin is more expensive but is taken in one dose.

Curable: Yes.

Syphilis

What it is: Bacterial infection.

What it does: If untreated, it can cause disease of the skin, bones, central nervous system, and heart.

How it's spread: During oral, anal, or vaginal sex; through deep kissing; or from a pregnant woman to her baby. Also, the sores it causes are highly infectious (meaning touching these sores at all is a really bad idea).

Symptoms: Syphilis affects the body in four phases: primary, secondary, latent, and late. Primary-phase (three to six weeks) symptoms include sores and open, wet ulcers. Secondary-phase (three weeks to two years) symptoms include swollen glands, a rash, tiredness, fever, sore throat, headaches, hoarseness, and loss of appetite. The latent phase begins after two years and has no symptoms, so the only way to detect the disease is through a blood test. Late phase is the name given to the long-term effects of syphilis, which can include brain damage, heart disease, and insanity.

Treatment: Penicillin or tetracycline.

Curable: Yes.

Gonorrhea

What it is: Bacterial infection.

What it does: If left untreated, it can cause pelvic inflammatory disease (PID) and sterility in women and a swollen penis and testicles in men. Both sexes may suffer from arthritis and skin problems.

How it's spread: Through oral, anal, or vaginal sex or from a pregnant woman to her fetus.

Symptoms: Often none, especially for women. Symptoms that may appear include burning during urination, oozing discharge, and infections in the throat or rectum.

Treatment: Penicillin or antibiotics taken in pill form or injected into your butt. Unfortunately, the disease is becoming increasingly resistant to known cures.

Curable: Yes.

Hepatitis (Types A, B, and C)

What it is: Hepatitis A, B, and C are three strains of the same disease, which is a highly contagious virus that attacks the liver. It can be acute (flaring up for two or three months, then never resurfacing again) or chronic (continually resurfacing). A is always acute, making it less harmful than the other two strains (although very rarely it can be serious, even life-threatening). B tends to be acute, but one single flare-up is often more severe than flare-ups of either A or C. C is often chronic, making serious long–term effects more likely.

What it does: In the mildest case, you may never know you have it, and the symptoms you do have may disappear completely in six months. But you can also contract it for life, in which case you can develop chronic liver disease or liver cancer. Short-term effects include fatigue, abdominal pain, loss of appetite, intermittent nausea, and vomiting.

How it's spread: A: Through infected food or water or contact with infected feces. B and C: Through exchange of semen, vaginal fluids, or saliva, usually during oral, anal, or vaginal sex and sometimes deep kissing. You can also get it by being exposed to an infected person's blood through cuts, open sores, blood transfusions, or sharing needles or other infected objects. All three strains can be transmitted from a pregnant woman to her baby.

Symptoms: Often nothing obvious. If you do show symptoms, some will be flulike, including fatigue and nausea, others include dark urine and yellowing of the eyes and skin.

Treatment: No cure. But symptoms can be alleviated with large amounts of rest and a high-protein, high-carbohydrate diet (to repair damaged cells). You can be vaccinated against hepatitis A and B, so ask your doctor about it. There is no vaccine for hepatitis C.

Curable: No, but A and B are preventable through vaccination.

Herpes

What it is: A virus. When the symptoms appear on or around the mouth, it's called oral herpes. When they appear near the genitals, it's called genital herpes.

What it does: Even when symptoms don't show up, you carry the virus in your blood forever.

How it's spread: Touching, kissing, and through vaginal, anal, or oral intercourse just before or during an outbreak of herpes sores. It can be passed from one partner to another or from one part of the body to another.

Symptoms: Oral herpes causes cold sores or fever blisters, which can be passed on through common contact but go away quickly. Genital herpes often shows no symptoms for long periods after it's contracted. The most common symptom of a herpes outbreak is a cluster of blistery sores, usually on the vagina, vulva, cervix, penis, or butt. These outbreaks can cause pain, itching, burning, and an inability to urinate; fever; chills; headache; swollen lymph glands in the groin, throat, and under the arms; and achy, flulike feelings. Generally the first outbreak is the most severe, and outbreaks get increasingly less severe as time goes on until they disappear altogether (usually after a number of years, depending on the person).

Treatment: There is no cure, but herpes can be transmitted only during a breakout or in the few days just before a breakout. There are prescription medications you can take during an outbreak and/or between outbreaks to keep the virus in check and help prevent its spread.

Curable: No.

Genital Warts (HPV)

What it is: A group of viruses that infect the skin. There are over seventy different strains of HPV.

What it does: Depending on the strain, it can cause warts on the genitals, warts on other parts of the body like the hands or feet, genital infections (which are often invisible), and internal growths.

How it's spread: Through skin-to-skin contact (usually vaginal, anal, or oral intercourse), whether or not warts are visible.

Symptoms: Often none. Sometimes soft, flesh-colored warts that look like cauliflower florets appear on the skin, especially near the genitals and mouth. They can appear in more than one place and often cluster in large masses (also, they may itch). If left untreated, the infectious growths can block the openings of the urethra, penis, and anus and cause sores, bleeding, and pain.

Treatment: There is no cure for the virus, but visible warts can be removed by applying chemicals directly to the growths, as with cryotherapy (which freezes them off), or with electrocauterization (which burns them off), or through surgery or lasers. Some people have recurring warts and need to undergo these treatments more than once.

Curable: No.

HIV/AIDS

What it is: A virus. Contracting HIV (human immunodeficiency virus) causes the onset of AIDS (acquired immune deficiency syndrome). AIDS is actually a collection of symptoms caused by the HIV virus and is sometimes referred to as the last stage of HIV disease.

What it does: The HIV virus breaks down the immune system, making it increasingly harder for the body to fight off disease. It leads to the development of harmful viral, bacterial, fungal, and parasitic infections—as well as a number of unusual cancers—all over the body. AIDS may also cause a person to develop HIV wasting syndrome (involuntary loss of 10 percent or more of normal weight); chronic diarrhea, weakness, and fever; thrush (a thick, whitish coating of the tongue or mouth that is sometimes accompanied by a sore throat); increased ease in bruising; recurring night sweats; increased shortness of breath; severe numbness or pain in the hands or feet; loss of muscle control and reflex; paralysis or loss of muscular strength; chronic pelvic inflammatory disease; swelling or hardening of glands in the throat, armpit, or groin; the appearance of discolored or purplish growths on the skin or inside the mouth; unexplained bleeding from growths on the skin, from mucus membranes, or from any opening in the body; recurring or unusual skin rashes; various forms of pneumonia; tuberculosis; cervical cancer; and death.

How it's spread: Through transmission of body fluids such as blood, semen, and vaginal fluids, usually during vaginal, oral, or anal sex, and through breast milk. It can also be transmitted by sharing infected needles or syringes, from a pregnant woman to her baby, or via a blood transfusion or organ donation.

Symptoms: Although some people show signs of the disease almost immediately, there may be no symptoms for ten years or more after a person is infected. When they do appear, early symptoms include unexplained weight loss, flulike symptoms, diarrhea, fatigue, persistent fevers, night sweats, headaches, mental disorders, and severe or recurring vaginal yeast infections.

Treatment: While drugs and drug treatments have been developed that slow the damage HIV does to the immune system, there is no cure. However, the earlier HIV is detected, the better treatments will work (although they are ineffective about 20 percent of the time).

Curable: No.

Note: Many STDs have no obvious symptoms, so you should get your blood tested at least once a year if you are sexually active—especially if you have more than one partner. Most doctors don't automatically test for STDs, so you've gotta bring it up.

is oral sex **safe?**

Hi, I had a question about a blow job. My boyfriend wants me to give him one. I was just wondering—is it possible to get an STD that way? Should I go down on him? I love him, and I know he loves me. I'm just not sure if I should do this or not.

I still am the Big V (virgin), but he's not. The last time he had sex was like a year ago. I'm really scared about this whole STD thing.

Sincerely,

—KELLY

HEY, KELLY,

Okay, first: Yes, you can get an STD that way. There may not be the generous variety of diseases you could get via genital-genital contact, and it may be a millifraction more difficult to contract one orally, but the risk is still totally there. Herpes, for instance. Hepatitis (all kinds). HIV. And, well, that's just the H's!

(Oh, and risk goes waaay up if you swallow his, uh, spooge. Know what I'm saying?)

Second: If you decide to go for it and want to cover your bases, use a condom. Sound gross? Luckily, you can get all kinds of flavors. Strawberry-banana. Chocolate. French vanilla.

Third: Should you do it? Here's what I think: If there's doubt in your

GETTING PROTECTION IS:
A breeze: 49%
Not that easy: 34%
Impossible: 6%
No answer: 11%

For the first time in history, sex is more dangerous than the cigarette

mind, pay very, very close attention to it. Break down the reasons you feel uncomfortable doing it. My guess is there are some pretty good ones in there.

Later.

fiona says

Yeah, you can definitely get all kinds of icky STDs from giving your guy a blow job—no matter how long it's been since he last had sex. And there's no way to tell if he's "clean" by just looking at him, either.

The bottom line: If you're going to be sexually active—in any way—you have to use protection every single time. So yes, that means making him wear a condom when you go down on him. And when you visit the gyno (you should be going once a year if you're having any kind of sex), be sure to get screened for STDs.

Tell him you're not up for herpes, and he's gotta get tested first.
—Alannah

I hope he's not pressuring you to blow him because that would suck. Get it? —Davey

afterward.—Jay Leno In 1962 the expression "safe sex"— all that

i think my bf gave me
herpes

I'm really worried that I might have herpes.

My boyfriend and I have been together for seven months, and I think he unknowingly gave it to me. He doesn't think he has anything, but he's the only one I've ever had sex with. I'm on birth control, and we've used condoms every time but once. I'm sure it was that one time that I got it. One time, just one time. That's not fair. I have friends who've had unprotected sex with more than ten people, and they're fine. So why me? Now people will automatically think that I'm slutty and dirty.

I just feel so overwhelmed, confused, and lost—and I don't know what to do next. I've made an appointment to get tested. But I don't even know why I'm sending this because there's nothing anyone can do to help me. My life is over. I'll never have anyone want to date me again.

—DIANE

tucker says

DEAR DIANE,

First of all, go get tested. Right away. It sounds like you don't know for sure what your situation is. Find out the truth, now.

But guess what? Even if you do have the herpes virus, your life isn't even close to over. Why? Because over 20 million people in America, and millions more all around the world, are living with herpes right now, thanks to good doctors and

meant then was you just move the bed from against the wall so you won't

good medicines. The fact is, even though it's a dangerous and unpleasant virus to have, it won't kill you. It won't even take you out of the dating pool. I promise.

Get to a doctor or clinic (check your yellow pages or surf on over to http://www.herpes.org), where you can find out the truth. Not only so you know where you stand, but also so you can learn about herpes and how to deal with it. It's not a death sentence—it's not even a "no-more-dating" sentence. That is, if you take care of it now.

There's a good chance that you don't have herpes. You could be totally healthy. Then again, you could have another sexually transmitted disease. Other STDs, like syphilis, have similar symptoms—but unlike herpes, they are curable. And the sooner you go in for treatment, the better. In the meantime, try not to beat yourself up too much about it. You made a mistake once, and you won't let it happen again.

Besides, that may not have even been when you contracted the virus—because even condoms don't offer full protection against its transmission.

Unlike other STDs, herpes can be spread just from rubbing against an infected person (with or without a condom). The virus can also be spread during kissing and vaginal, anal, and oral contact.

Get tested.

If he's pretty sure that he doesn't have anything, then maybe it's not herpes. —sweetie

Many people who have herpes never show symptoms, so get tested now. —Angelica

bang your head.—David Letterman The percentage of sexually

my bf is offended that
i'm scared of stds

I've been going out with my boyfriend for about two months now. I'm a virgin—he's not. I really do love him, though, and he says he loves me. But last night he asked me about sex. I told him I was scared of getting an STD, and he flipped out. I really didn't expect that.

He's 17, I'm only 15, so I thought he'd understand. Instead he got really offended. He thinks that only dirty and slutty people get STDs. I told him that's not true, but he just wouldn't listen. Now he's not talking to me, and I just wanna die.

What can I tell him to make him understand? There's no way I wanna break up with him or anything, so please try and avoid suggesting that.

—BRIE

DEAR BRIE,

Okay, you don't have to break up with your boyfriend, but you do need to slap some sense into him. After all, he's older than you and he doesn't realize that he's just as susceptible to getting an STD as anyone else. That's just dumb.

You are not a terrible person for being concerned about getting a disease. You're just smart.

Should you decide to have sex with him down the road (it's good that you're talking about it, but there's no need to rush . . .), do whatever you think is necessary to feel good about that decision. Make him get tested, and insist that he wear a condom every time.

tucker says

First, props on bringing it up with him. Talking about sex and STDs isn't easy.

Now, lemme let you in on a little secret. He said this so he won't have to wear a condom. In fact, guys will say all kinds of things to avoid wearing a condom. They'll say, "But I'm allergic to latex!" which is true about 1 percent of the time. They'll say, "I'll take it out before I pop," (hello, ever heard of precum?).

The most effective, and most dangerous, thing they'll say is, "You don't trust me! How can you think I'd have something?" The reason this one is the worst is because it turns the whole thing back on you.

Time to throw down a big, major rule: No rubber-free nookie. Period. No discussion. If he respects your rule (and if he's a smart guy, he will), then you can move forward. If he doesn't, you're on a quick path to a breakup anyway. . . . He'll be disrespecting you, you'll be mad at him, you'll be mad at yourself for putting up with him, and so on.

Pressuring you into having unsafe sex is just as bad as pressuring you into having unwanted sex. Got it?

> ARE YOU CONCERNED ABOUT GETTING AN STD?
> Not even: 12%
> A little, but not really: 33%
> Totally: 43%
> No answer: 12%

You need to lose that boy and find yourself a man. —Randall

If you ask me, he's just this side of raping you. —aliz

49.9 percent in 1999, while condom use among sexually active

can **condoms** fall off?

I've got a question. When you have sex, can a condom fall off inside you? And if it does, can the sperm spill inside you?
—CURIOUS

tucker says

DEAR CURIOUS,

Yes, and yes. The thing about condoms is, they're really, really effective if you use them correctly. If you don't, they could break, or fall off, or otherwise get you into all kinds of trouble.

So, here's how:

1. Open the package carefully. Don't rip the condom, just the package. Do not use your teeth or scissors.

2. As you roll it on gently, make sure the rolled-up part is on the outside, and squeeze the slack at the top so there's no air in it (this will leave an empty space for all the "discharge" to go). Start at the head of the penis and work your way all the way to the base. Don't tug or pull. Besides causing pain for the poor guy, this could tear the condom.

3. After you've had sex, the fella's got to pull out before his erection goes down, and (this is important) he should hold the condom at the base while he's pulling out to make sure it doesn't come off inside. He should check it every now and then during the deed, too, to make sure it's still on.

4. And if you're using any lubricant, don't use an oil-based one. You know, like baby oil or anything. It breaks down latex big time (you might as well be poking it with pins and needles). Use a water-based one like K-Y or Astroglide.

If you're gonna do it, do it right.

students increased from 46 percent to 58 percent. As late as 1965, pre-

mona says

Yep, condoms aren't 100 percent foolproof. That's why if you're having sex, you should seriously think about using a backup method of birth control—like the pill—in addition to condoms.

And that's why you should make smart decisions about who you sleep with in general. 'Cause if your condom breaks (or falls off, or whatever), there goes your protection against STDs and AIDS.

On the pregnancy prevention tip, though, there are things you can do if the condom falls off or breaks. If you visit your doctor or a Planned Parenthood clinic within seventy-two hours of the mishap, you can get a prescription for emergency contraception, a special combination of birth control pills that can reduce your chances of becoming pregnant by about 75 percent.

Know that emergency contraception is harsh on your body. It can have short-term side effects like severe nausea, dizziness, and irregular bleeding —so you shouldn't think of it as birth control. Think of it more as a last resort.

But it's a much better option than going through an unwanted pregnancy or an abortion.

P.S.—If, after you've had sex, you suspect something's gone wrong with your condom (like it broke), get to the bottom of it right away. Both you and your partner should take a good, hard look at it—as a team—and determine whether or not you need to bug.

I seriously hope you're planning on sharing these instructions with your boyfriend. —danita

Use a condom AND spermicide, and you'll feel safer. —cure

your
protection options

The best way to avoid getting pregnant or contracting a disease is to not have sex. But, we know that abstinence is not always the method of choice. That means you should protect yourself. Here's a list of the top ways to stay healthy and pregnancy free.

The Condom

How it works: Before sexual contact, you put a condom over the penis, creating a barrier so pre-ejaculatory fluid and ejaculate never get near any potentially dangerous places.

Effectiveness against pregnancy: 86% to 98% (it's on the higher end if you use them right).

Why they're good: They're cheap and easy to find, they're small and you can carry them around, and they're better for preventing pregnancy than most other protection options (especially when used in conjunction with spermicide or the birth control pill). Seriously, condoms are the best protection there is, besides abstinence, against HIV and other STDs.

Why they might suck: When they break, they don't protect against anything; you have to remember to put them on in the heat of the moment; some people are allergic to latex and spermicide; and there can be a loss of sensation, especially for guys.

Your rights: You don't need anyone's permission to get condoms, and you can buy them at any drugstore—no matter how old you are (they're also given out, free of charge or at a discount, at many clinics, county health centers, and some high school health departments).

Depo-Provera

How it works: Depo-Provera is the brand name for a shot of the hormone depo-medroxyprogesterone (DMPA). A doctor gives you a shot of it every 12 weeks in the arm, hip, or buttocks. It keeps the ovaries from releasing eggs and also prevents sperm from joining with eggs.

Effectiveness against pregnancy: 99.7%.

Why it's good: It has a very low failure rate; it starts working immediately if you receive the shot within the first five days of your period; it protects against ovarian and endometrial cancer; it reduces menstrual cramps; it helps prevent anemia; once you get it, you don't have to think about birth control for three months; for most women, menstrual bleeding decreases over time and may even disappear after years of use.

Why it might suck: You have to make sure to get the shots regularly—if you are more than two weeks late for your next shot, you may have to have a pregnancy test before getting another; it offers no protection against STDs; most women experience irregular menstrual bleeding, especially during the first three to six months of use; each shot costs approximately $35, plus the doctor's visit ($15 to $120, depending on your doctor and your insurance); it may have side effects like dizziness, nausea, depression, increased appetite and weight gain, increased face or body hair, and hair loss. Also, it's been shown to contribute to bone loss.

Your rights: You must visit a doctor to get it, and, depending on where you live, you may need parental permission if you're under 18.

Diaphragm

How it works: You put spermicide on a dome-shaped rubber cup with a flexible rim and insert it into the vagina, as per package instructions. This keeps sperm from getting past the cervix to the egg.

Effectiveness against pregnancy: 80% to 94%.

Why it's good: It can be inserted up to six hours before sex and can be left in for twenty-four hours; it can be reused and used twice in one night without being removed (as long as you reapply spermicide); it usually can't be felt by either partner; it may reduce the risk of cervical cancer; it lasts about two years.

Why it might suck: You have to be fitted for one by a doctor; it can be expensive (about $80 to $150, including the doctor's visit); it can be difficult to insert and easy to insert wrong; it may become dislodged if the woman is on top during sex; it doesn't protect effectively against STDs; you can be allergic to the spermicide; if you leave it in for more than twenty-four hours, you can develop toxic shock syndrome; you have to keep it in for six hours after sex and then wash it thoroughly.

Your rights: You must see a doctor to be fitted for a diaphragm.

Female Condom

How it works: You insert a tubelike plastic sheath with flexible rings at each end deep into the vagina, as per package instructions. The ring at the closed end holds it in place, while the ring at the open end remains outside the vagina. Semen collects inside the condom, preventing it from entering the vagina.

Effectiveness against pregnancy: 79% to 95%.

Why it's good: It's cheap (about $2.50 per condom), it can be bought over the counter, it can be used by people who are allergic to spermicide, you can insert it up to eight hours before having sex, and it protects against STDs.

Why it might suck: It may cause irritation of the vagina or penis; it may slip; it's hard to use; it may decrease sensation for the girl; it has to be removed immediately after sex, before you stand up, or sperm can slip around it. It is also less effective than the male condom.

Your rights: The female condom is available over the counter, and there is no minimum age to purchase one.

Morning-After Pill
(Emergency Contraception)

How it works: If something goes wrong with your normal use of contraception (like a condom broke or you missed too many pills this month) or if you didn't protect yourself during sex, you can go to a clinic and get a pill that contains an extra-strong dose of hormones that protect against pregnancy.

Effectiveness against pregnancy: 75% (the closer you are to ovulation, the less effective it is).

Why it's good: If you screw up (or if your protection fails), it's a last-ditch method to try to avoid getting pregnant.

Why it might suck: It can cause severe nausea, vomiting, and cramping; it doesn't protect against STDs; it can be hard to get, especially if there are no nearby health clinics. It's a last-ditch method, as mentioned, and should not be relied on as a regular form of birth control.

Your rights: You must obtain a doctor's prescription to get it, and, depending on where you live, you may need parental permission if you're under 18.

Norplant

How it works: Six flexible plastic rods, each about the size of a cardboard match, are surgically inserted under your skin on your upper arm. They time release the hormone levonorgestrel (a type of progestin), which keeps the ovaries from releasing eggs and prevents sperm from joining with eggs. One set of implants lasts five years.

Effectiveness against pregnancy: 99%.

Why it's good: It lasts five years, so you don't have to think about birth control for a long time; it starts working within twenty-four hours of insertion; it helps prevent uterine cancer.

Why it might suck: It's expensive ($450 to $900 for insertion of the rods, $90 to $300 for removal); the rods may be visible; it doesn't protect against any STDs; it may leave a scar; it causes changes in most women's menstrual cycle (which may include irregular intervals between periods, a longer or heavier menstrual flow, irregular bleeding or spotting between periods, and/or not getting your period for months at a time); it may have side effects including headache, change in appetite, weight gain or loss, depression, dizziness, nervousness, sore breasts, and nausea.

Your rights: You must see a doctor to get it, and, depending on where you live, you may need parental permission if you're under 18.

The Pill 8

How it works: The girl takes one hormone pill every day. There are several different kinds, and each works in a different way. Because they mess with your body chemistry, you need to have a doctor check you out to determine which will work best for you.

Effectiveness against pregnancy: 95% to 99.9% (depending on the type of pill you take and how good you are about taking it regularly).

Why it's good: If taken every day at the same time, the pill is highly effective in preventing unwanted pregnancy; it can regulate your periods; decrease PMS symptoms like acne, cramping, bloating, and iron deficiency; and help prevent cancer and other diseases. Plus—no potential for heat-of-the-moment forgetting.

Why it might suck: It's expensive ($10 to $30 a month) and is not covered by all insurance carriers; if not taken regularly it doesn't work; it doesn't prevent STDs; potential temporary side effects include bloating, increased breast size, weight gain, and spotting (irregular bleeding in small amounts outside of the normal menstrual flow); smokers on the pill have a greatly increased risk of heart disease.

Your rights: To get on the pill, you need to get a prescription from a doctor or clinic—and, depending on where you live, you may need parental permission if you're under 18.

Spermicide

How it works: As per package instructions, you insert it deep into the vagina (it's available in foams, creams, jellies, or suppositories). It kills the sperm before they have a chance to reach the egg.

Effectiveness against pregnancy: 72% to 94%.

Why it's good: It's cheap ($4 to $18) and can be used along with other methods for increased protection. Spermicides also kill some germs that spread STDs.

Why it might suck: It may cause irritation of the penis as well as vaginal and yeast infections; it can be messy; many people are allergic; on its own it doesn't reliably protect against STDs.

Your rights: Spermicides can be bought over the counter, no matter how old you are.

Sponge (aka the Today Sponge)

How it works: It's a small sponge that contains the spermicide nonoxynol-9. You moisten it with water and insert it deep into the vagina as per package instructions. The spermicide kills most of the sperm; the sponge is supposed to block the rest.

Effectiveness against pregnancy: 89% to 91% if used correctly.

Why it's good: It protects against pregnancy for up to twenty-four hours without the need to refresh the spermicide, no matter how many times you have sex; it's comfortable; it's cheap (about $2 per sponge); it's small and can be carried in your purse, just like a condom.

Why it might suck: It doesn't protect against the spread of STDs; it's less effective than most other forms of contraception; you can be allergic to the spermicide; it's easy to insert incorrectly.

Your rights: You can buy the sponge over the counter (without a prescription) at any age.

Note: The sponge was taken off the market in 1995 because its manufacturer, Whitehall-Robins Healthcare, discovered problems in its manufacturing process (there was no medical reason for the sponge to be removed from the market). In 1999 Allendale Pharmaceuticals bought the patent and made plans to manufacture and market the sponge once again. Check out Today's website, www.todaysponge.com, for more information.

i'm scared to get
tested for HIV

I'm 18, and I've had a lot of unprotected sex. With several girls. I just found out that I have an STD. I got it taken care of, but my doctor told me that I should probably get an HIV test. I told her that I couldn't deal yet.

The thing is, I'm scared. I really think I may be HIV positive. I've slept around so much and haven't been careful at all.

I know I should take the test—just to know. But I have so many questions. What is the test like? Can I do the test myself? And is there a way I can keep my results confidential?

Please write back.

—FREAKING

tucker says

DEAR FREAKING,

Sounds like you had a nice, big fat reality check the other day at the doctor's. Ouch. I'll save the "Dude, what were you thinking!" because it sounds like you already said that to yourself.

But I will encourage you to find out your status, now. Because the sooner you know, the sooner you can do something about it.

Here's what happens when you go for an HIV test: You go to the doctor or to a clinic, and they draw some blood from your arm. Frankly, it's not that big a deal.

What IS a big deal is waiting for the results. A true reading takes several days. See, they do more than one test to make sure

114

HAVE YOU EVER
HAD AN HIV TEST?
Yes: 13%
No: 75%
No answer: 12%

the info they're giving you is correct. Sure, some doctors or clinics will give you results the same day, but because the quick-result system can give you a false reading, it's much smarter to wait for the real story. I know someone who thought he was HIV positive after the quick result but after further testing found out he was HIV negative. He was relieved, but it was a nightmare.

There are at-home test kits that you can use—you prick your finger, then send the blood through the mail to a testing center, but it's too easy to screw them up (on your side and theirs), so I don't recommend them.

Best bet: Hit a local clinic where you can get tested anonymously. (Not just confidentially, but anonymously.) Many places offer this—be sure to ask right up front. "Anonymous" means you never have to give your name or age or anything. . . . They assign you a number, and you go back to the clinic after four or five days, read off your number, and get your results. They never even know who you are. "Confidential" means they keep a record (which they say no one can ever see—but I say, so why keep a record?). Go for anonymous.

Any decent clinic will talk you through the whole process, with trained counselors, so you don't feel like you're bugging the whole time. Call (800) 342-AIDS to find a clinic in your area.

The bad news about being HIV positive: There is no cure, and it's very, very likely that you'll have HIV for the rest of your life. The (sort of) good news: For many people, there are treatments available that can keep you healthy, and the sooner you know the truth, the more effective these can be.

But know this: These treatments don't work for everyone, and they aren't a cure . . . no matter what you've heard.

Go do it, man. Do it soon. It's better to know than to wonder and assume the worst.

The prospect of being tested for HIV is super-scary. But it's definitely better to know your HIV status than to just sit around wondering about it. If you're HIV negative, then you've been torturing yourself for no reason. And if you're positive, you're not getting treatment that could help you.

Like Tucker said, there are measures you can take to make sure that no one but you will ever know the results of your test. 'Cause let's face it, people who are HIV positive or who have full-blown AIDS are still discriminated against in our society, as wrong as that may be.

So I say, do what you gotta do. Go to a clinic, get an anonymous test, get another test six months later (this is rec-ommended because HIV tests actually test for antibodies against HIV and it can take up to six months after exposure to the virus for the body to produce those antibodies). If you're negative, you can breathe a huge sigh of relief—and make a fresh start by never having unsafe sex again.

And if you come up positive, then you need to talk to a counselor about what your options are. Having HIV is a major, life-changing issue to deal with. But with new advances in treatments, many people living with HIV and AIDS are living longer than ever before.

Take the test so if you are HIV positive, you can't spread it to anyone else. —January

Actually, I'm worried about the girls
that you've been with.—West

cases of HIV infection were reported worldwide in 1999.

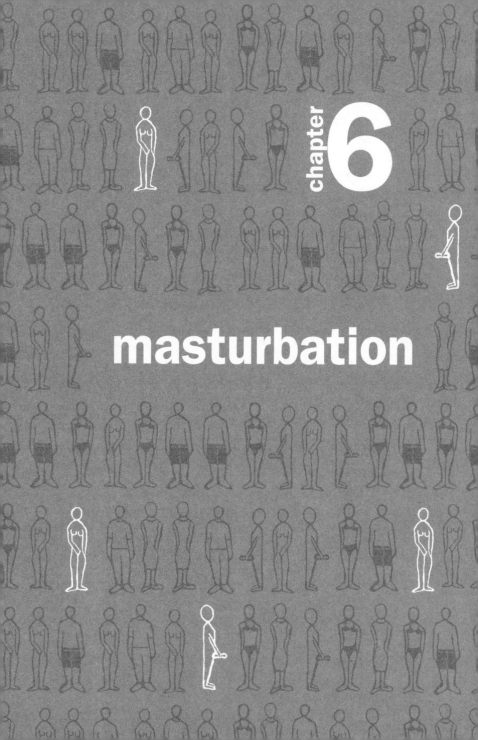

masturbation

We all do it. Okay, if you say you don't, fine. I'm not gonna push it. What if I say it this way: We're all interested in it. Okay, if you say you aren't, fine.

But the point is, masturbation is one of those things that a lot of people just can't deal with discussing. Why? Because it's a little embarrassing, it's a little PG-13 . . . and it's incredibly personal.

But hey, it's also incredibly safe, which is no small potatoes. That's why we sandwiched this section between STDs and Pregnancy. It's the absolute best, surefire way to avoid both of these things while still gratifying yourself sexually.

So, feel free to read this section on the down-low. Or read it out loud to your friends, whatever.

Just have fun with it.

tucker

i **masturbate.** a lot

I have a question. I am 14, and I masturbate one to three times a day. Is there anything wrong with that? Will it affect me when I am older? Please reply. Thank you for your time.
—JOHN

tucker says

DEAR JOHN,

Nope, nothing wrong with that.
Nope, it won't affect you when you're older.
Trust me, I know.
Carry on.

P.S.: Don't stress about it. Believe me, you won't keep up this pace forever.

fiona says

Forget the taboos about masturbation—the fact is that it's, like, the only way to get sexual satisfaction without risking someone getting pregnant or getting an STD. So how can that be bad? It can't.

So don't worry about it. You won't get zits or hairy palms or any other bodily weirdness—masturbation is not harmful in any way. At all. And it's totally normal.

DO YOU MASTURBATE?
Yep: 47%
Nope: 46%
No answer: 7%

About 5.5 million people are infected with genital warts each year. In

So as Tucker said, go on about your business. You're not hurting yourself—or anyone else.

Lata.

Despite what everyone says about masturbation, you know that they do it, too. —girlstar

Okay, I understand that everyone masturbates. But why do we have to talk about it all the time? —darla

IF YOU MASTURBATE, HOW OFTEN DO YOU DO IT?
More than once a day: 9%
Daily: 12%
A few times a week: 36%
Every couple of weeks or so: 28%
Almost never: 15%

oung people between the ages of 13 and 19, a much greater proportion of HIV

will masturbating affect the size of my penis?

I was just wondering . . . If you jack off a lot, will your penis increase in size?

—JOEY

tucker says

DEAR JOEY,

No. Believe me, I have some experience in this matter, and the answer is no.

In fact, there's no way to increase your size unless you get an implant. Which is a little desperate, if you ask me.

Once you hit your early twenties, you're about as big as you're gonna get. I'm guessing you haven't reached that age yet, so you've probably got a few years to grow.

fiona says

Yep, masturbating isn't going to make your penis any bigger. But hey, it's not going to make it smaller, either. And it's a good way to get to know your body.

So, uh, keep going about your business.

Go for it. Just make sure you're alone when you do. I got busted by my sister. —Allan

Yeah, dude. Your penis is gonna get like four times as big. Go masturbate more. —randall

infections was reported among females (62%) than among males (38%).

what's the big deal?

chicks masturbate!

Okay, I'll admit it. I'm a girl, and I masturbate.

But what I don't get is why everyone makes such an issue out of it. I mean, guys do it all the time, so why is it so shocking that a girl, uh, gives herself a hand every once in a while?

The other day, when I admitted to my friends that I liked to do it, all the girls pretended to be grossed out, and the guys got all into it. Eww. What's up with that?

—HONEST GAL

DEAR HONEST GAL,

What's up? It's simple. As with many sex-related subjects, when it comes to self-love, there's a serious double standard between guys and girls.

Guys are expected to be total horn dogs who "need" physical satisfaction—so they're allowed to masturbate. Girls, on the other hand, supposedly don't have the same "needs" — they can just wait for the right person to come along without "needing" to gratify themselves in the meantime. And by this logic, any girl who masturbates, well, she must have one helluva sex drive. Or so the double standard goes . . .

That's why the guys were all intrigued. Yeah, eww. And that's why the girls were trying to be all prim and properly grossed out—even though they most likely do it, too.

Or maybe they don't do it, just because they think they

aren't supposed to. Which is silly.

Props for being honest about it. Your friends could learn a thing or two from you.

Lata.

tucker says

Okay, I'm blushing.

Uh, yeah, from what I hear, girls do it just as much as guys. And yeah, it turns guys on to know that. Double standard or no, it's still gonna turn guys on.

One thing about masturbating, though—even though there's nothing wrong with it, it's a very personal, individual thing. That's why most people keep it to themselves and why broadcasting it makes other people all uncomfortable. Besides, there's no real reason to shout it from the rooftops.

Carry on.

If that's your thing, do what you gotta do! —chicklet

Yeah, I do it once in a while. I've never actually told anyone, though. —patootie

masturbation:
ew! or yeeha!

You gotta get to know your own body. People who don't know their own bodies are at the mercy of their partners (no matter how clumsy or incapable) when it comes to sex! And that sucks. —TrinaT

I totally think it's gross! I did it once and did NOT like it. —Lakergirl

Every guy in the whole world beats off. I usually do it in the shower. —HeadBanger

Hey, c'mon, it's okay to masturbate! I do it, and it's great! I'm not ashamed of it. Don't let anyone tell you that you're disgusting or whatever—they know they do it. —KornChik

pregnancy

No matter how careful you are about using birth control, if you're sexually active, there is a chance that you will become pregnant. Unless you're a guy, of course. But hey, if you are, keep reading—each year about 1 million American teenagers get pregnant and that means approximately 1 million guys are equally responsible for helping to cause those pregnancies.

The sad fact is, no method of birth control—except abstinence—is 100 percent effective.

Of course, if you're sexually active, your odds of becoming pregnant can be lowered with the use of contraceptives. Doubling up, using both a hormonal method (like the birth control pill) and a barrier method (like condoms or a diaphragm), is a highly effective way to prevent unwanted pregnancy. But it isn't foolproof.

If you do get pregnant, you'll have a lot of serious issues to deal with, but you do have other options besides premature motherhood. Like adoption or abortion. As scary as pregnancy and everything that goes along with it is, the sooner you find out whether or not you're really pregnant, the more choices you'll have.

And remember, while it takes two people to tango, only one can actually get pregnant. So, ladies, don't leave it to your partner to make the big decisions about birth control. You've got to take care of you.

home **pregnancy** tests

Last weekend my boyfriend and I had sex. Twice. The first time we used a condom. The second time we didn't. I have heard that if you have sex once, then the second time you won't get pregnant. Is this true?

I am starting to get scared. And what is the average time when you can tell from a home pregnancy test? Help!!!

—SCARED IN VIRGINIA

HEY, SCARED,

I suggest going to a clinic and getting a test as soon as possible, but keep the following fact in mind—you've got to wait until you've missed your period. That's because the tests aren't always sensitive enough to pick up the levels of human chorionic gonadotropin (HCG, the hormone that indicates that you're pregnant) at the very, very beginning of a pregnancy, when the levels of HCG in your blood and urine are low. Home pregnancy tests, in particular, can give you a false negative if you take them within just a few days of getting pregnant.

So as soon as you miss your period, see a pro and get a lab test (clinics like Planned Parenthood offer confidential testing at reduced prices—sometimes even free—for teens).

Seriously, do it right away—within a day or two of your missed period if you possibly can. Don't just sit around waiting—and praying—for your period. Taking a pregnancy test is definitely scary, but the sooner you get tested, the sooner

85% of teen pregnancies are unintended. The maximum depth at

you'll know what your options are and the more options you'll have.

tucker says

Go find that person who told you that you couldn't get pregnant on the second round and slap him/her upside the head with a nice, raw reality check.

Ouch!

See, you had the wrong info. And since you had the wrong info, you ran a risk. Not only a risk of pregnancy, either. Try every STD you can name, plus all the ones you've never even heard of. So don't do it again, okay?

We've all been there. Luckily, we never have to go back.

Later.

If I was you, I would tell your parents 'cause they will be a whole lot madder if they find out another way. —Lidia

I don't trust those at-home tests. Mine said I wasn't pregnant, but I am. Now I don't know what to do. —mandygirl

which vaginal stimulation occurs is 2 inches. One in nine women aged

can i get **pregnant** through clothes?

My BF and I fool around a lot with our clothes on. Can I get pregnant by rubbing against him with all our clothes on? Just wondering.

—ANONYMOUS

DEAR ANON,

Nah. And can I just say, rock on? A little rubby-rubby action with the clothes on is one of the best ways to do it without doing it. It's way safe, way sexy, and way fun. People have been doing it for centuries as an alternative to the real deal. But if you ask me, it's not just an alternative to something else—it's a full-on great thing all by itself.

Some people call it petting. I don't because that's what I do to the cat. Some people call it dry sex. I don't because that sounds so unfun. You call it whatever you want.

As with any activity, sexual or otherwise, don't do anything you don't want to do, and don't let your BF pressure you (and don't you pressure him) to go any further than you'd like to. But if it's cool with everyone involved, rub on.

tucker says

The cool thing about having outercourse—as opposed to intercourse—is that since you and your guy aren't having direct genital contact or exchanging any fluids, you don't have to worry as much about pregnancy or sexually transmitted diseases. Whew! What a relief, right?

And I don't know about you, but for me, making out is a lot more fun when you don't have to deal with superheavy worries going through your head.

Enjoy your peace of mind.

I think that it's cool that you're leaving the clothes on. It's a great way to show your commitment without giving the nookie. —FrotOn

I do this all the time and I have never gotten pregnant. So go with the flow! —katieb

should i tell my bf?

Well, I was dating this guy for like six months, and we thought really hard about having sex and made sure we did everything right before we did it. We finally did, but I THINK the condom broke. My period is late, and it's been two months since my last one. I haven't said anything to my BF about it because I'm scared he'll dump me.

Should I just wait to see what happens? Or should I inform my BF? Please help.

—KIRBY

fiona says

HEY, KIRBY,

Getting dumped by your BF is the least of your worries.

Right now, you've got to think of yourself first. And what you're going to do if you are, in fact, pregnant. The first order of business: going to a doctor and getting a pregnancy test so you can know what your status is. There is a chance that you're not pregnant—especially since you're young, and your periods may not be totally regular yet. But you should find out for sure.

If you do turn out to be pregnant, you may want to tell your boyfriend. But think about yourself first.

And realize that if you are pregnant, ultimately the decision of what you do is up to you.

tucker says

It's totally your choice (remember that!), but if I were your boyfriend, I'd want you to tell me.

I mean, if I was there, I'd want to know. And I have to say, horror stories aside, most guys feel the same way.

Sure, you always hear about guys ditching their girlfriends when they get pregnant or whatever, or guys who deny everything, or guys who just give their girlfriends some cash (for an abortion, I guess) and bolt, but most guys aren't like that.

Most of us, especially if we're six months or so into a relationship, will help you out if you ask. It sounds to me like this dude is like that—I mean, you-all waited, you thought really hard about things and talked about it, you "did everything right." So why not believe that he'll continue to "do everything right"?

Besides, if you really believe he'll freak and/or dump you, why would you want to be with him?

Good luck. And get a pregnancy test right away. Do not wait one more day. You've gotta know.

P.S.—If you're ever unsure about whether a condom has broken or not, you should check it out for holes when the guy takes it off. That way you'll know if there's a problem ASAP.

He has the right to know if he's going to have a kid. —Lily

If he does bolt, then he could never be a good, responsible father. —Angel

can you get pregnant from
oral sex?

Can you get pregnant from giving a guy oral sex . . . and swallowing??? I am freaked out now because I did and people are telling me that you CAN get pregnant.

—ANONYMOUS

DEAR ANONYMOUS,

No, you can't get pregnant from swallowing semen. (Can I just say that I hate that word?)

So you're in the clear. On the pregnancy tip, that is. But when it comes to HIV and a whole slew of other STDs, you're on thin ice. In early 2000, the U.S. government released a study showing that HIV infection rates are going up—especially among teens—and that unprotected oral sex is one of the reasons.

See, if you have even the tiniest scrape or cut or sore or whatever in your mouth—even so small that you don't feel it (like if you brushed your teeth too hard that morning)—his semen (and everything in it, viruses, bacteria, and fungus, oh my!) hits your bloodstream directly. Instant infection. (Not just HIV, either—try herpes, hepatitis, syphilis, gonorrhea, etc., etc., etc.).

fiona says

In order for you to become pregnant, a sperm must fertilize one of your eggs (which can only happen through the vagina), and the fertilized egg has to implant itself in the wall

to a mere 14. Historians believe that it was dementia caused by of your uterus. That's Reproduction 101.

But if that sounds like Latin to you—instead of, like, basic info about your own body—it's time to pay closer attention in sex ed. Or to pick up a book like *Our Bodies, Ourselves for the New Century.* Or both. The bottom line is that you shouldn't be engaging in sexual activity—of any kind—if you don't understand your body and how it works. So start schoolin' yourself.

> **GIRLS: IF YOU HAVE BEEN PREGNANT, HOW DID YOU DEAL WITH IT?**
> Still have my baby: 45%
> Gave it up for adoption: 12%
> Had an abortion: 43%

> **GIRLS: HAVE YOU EVER BEEN PREGNANT?**
> Yeah: 6%
> Nope: 94%

If you consider that oral sex usually leads to full-on sex, then the answer is yes. —Dr.K

News flash! Your mouth is not connected to your uterus!
—Bama

syphilis that led to Vincent Van Gogh's madness and eventual suicide.

what can i expect if i have an
abortion?

I'm 16 years old, and I just found out that I'm pregnant. It's early on—I found out this week, after only being just over a week late for my period—so I know I have a lot of choices.

But I know that no matter what happens, I am going to have an abortion. I'm way too young to become a parent—I haven't even finished high school yet. That's why my boyfriend and I were using condoms in the first place.

My question is, how can I get one, and what should I expect outta the whole deal—physically and emotionally? And should I tell my boyfriend about it?

—ABBY

DEAR ABBY,

fiona says

Wow. Deciding to have an abortion has to be one of the toughest choices you'll have to make in your life.

But luckily, you do have the choice. In this country, it is your legal right to obtain an abortion to end an unwanted pregnancy. However, since you're under 18, you may need to get a parent or guardian's consent before you can have an abortion.

The laws regarding this vary from state to state, so contact your local Planned Parenthood (call 800-230-PLAN for the location nearest you) to find out what the situation is in your state. Planned Parenthood can also refer you to doctors and clinics that are licensed to perform the procedure.

Before you can obtain an abortion, you have to have

several tests—a pregnancy test to confirm that you're pregnant, a blood test to screen for anemia, and a pelvic exam. By
law, you also must receive counseling to inform you of all
your options—having a baby and keeping it, having a baby
and giving it up for adoption, and having an abortion.

If you decide to go through with the abortion, you'll have
to sign a form acknowledging that you've been informed of
all your options and of the risks associated with the procedure (just like any medical procedure, there are risks—but an
early abortion is eleven times safer than giving birth) and
that you have chosen to have an abortion of your own free
will.

The usual method of early abortion (performed within the
first three months of pregnancy) is referred to as suction
curettage. The actual procedure takes about ten to fifteen
minutes. Here's what happens:

*Your vagina is washed with an antiseptic.

*You receive a local anesthetic, usually injected in or near
your cervix.

*The opening of your cervix is gradually stretched, using
a series of increasingly thick rods called dilators. (The thick-
est is about the width of a pen.)

*After the cervical opening is stretched, a tube is inserted
into the uterus.

*The tube is attached to a suction machine, which emp-
ties the uterus. After the tube is removed, a narrow metal
loop called a curette is used to scrape the walls of the uterus
to ensure that it's been completely emptied.

Afterward you will rest in a recovery room for as long as
you need (usually an hour or so). You'll be observed to make

at which the erotic sensations travel from the skin to the brain has been

sure that you're okay and haven't suffered any complications. Then the clinic will give you instructions for taking care of yourself after the procedure, as well as a twenty-four-hour emergency number to call in case complications arise. You'll also have to schedule a follow-up appointment for from two to four weeks after you've had the abortion.

Generally the recovery time is short. Although you shouldn't engage in strenuous physical activity for a while afterward, you can usually return to school or work the following day. Most women experience cramps and menstrual-like bleeding for a few days to a couple of weeks after the procedure. But severe pain, heavy bleeding, and fever are abnormal symptoms—so if you have these, you need to contact your doctor ASAP.

Now you've got the facts, Abby. It's up to you to make the choice that is right for you. But if you do decide that you want to have an abortion, don't put it off—the further your pregnancy progresses, the greater the risk of complications.

tucker says

I don't know about you, but my head's spinnin' already! Sounds like a gnarly thing to go through.

Luckily, these days abortion is an incredibly safe and effective procedure, and many, many people have them every single day. (Each year approximately 1.5 million American women have abortions.) And I bet you'd never guess how many people close to you have gone through it. There are billions of places on the Web to talk to people about it, to find out more about it, all that stuff. So whatever you decide, you can find support.

And doing this won't be easy, you'll need the support.

All that aside, here's the first thing you need to do:

Remind yourself that this is your decision. No one else's.
Now, should you tell your boyfriend? Only you can answer
that. Ask yourself, "Will telling him truly, truly be helpful to me
right now?" Think hard, and think deep. If the answer is 100
percent yes, then I think you should reach out to him. But if
you have any inkling at all that he won't rise to the occasion
(as in, act like a man), then you might want to hold back.

In fact, whenever you have to make a choice about telling
anyone you're close to—friends, family, etc.—you should ask
yourself that same question. This is your show, so you get to
decide how to run it. Okay?

As a guy and a boyfriend, I'd really want to know. I'd really
want to be able to be there to help out. And I know I would.
(Note to all boyfriends . . . check your brain: Would you be
supportive no matter what? Would you?) Frankly, I think most
guys feel the same way. But at a time like this, teenage guys—
hey, people in general—don't always act like they should. Sad
to say, many girls in your situation have been dissed hard by
their guys. You might not want to set yourself up for that—
you've got enough to deal with already.

In the meantime, and right away, find someone to help
you handle whatever you decide to do—a girlfriend, a family
member, a counselor, an e-mail pal, someone.

There you have it, Abby. Remember this, though: No matter what happens, you've got to do what's right for you.

a girl's life is worth more than a fetus. and a fetus is not a person—it
is a cluster of cells. so you should respect her choice. besides, there
are enough unwanted children in the world already. —Alannah.

I mean, there are tons of people who can't have kids and want
to adopt—why don't you think about doing that? —g-girl

thinks it's foreplay.—Susan Sarandon in *Bull Durham* Teenagers in

my gf had an abortion and
didn't tell me

My girlfriend and I have been together for over a year, and we've been having sex for almost the whole time. She just told me that three months ago she had an abortion.

I didn't know what to say.

I'm not upset that she got an abortion. I mean, I know it's her choice, and to be honest, I'm glad she chose abortion, for her and for me, but . . . I was the one who got her pregnant, and I can't help being pissed that she didn't tell me what was going on.

I don't want to get into a fight about it, but I feel like I had a right to know. Did I?

—AMIGO

tucker says

DEAR AMIGO,

Not really.

Straight-up fact: Preventing pregnancy is everyone's job. But a pregnancy that's already in full effect is under a woman's control. She bears the child; she calls the shots. She has the responsibility, so she also gets to make the decisions. That includes who she tells and when.

Still, I'm down with where you're coming from. I mean, you had a lot to do with her situation, and it sounds like you would have been helpful and supportive.

There are a million reasons a girl wouldn't tell her man. Being a guy, I can't even imagine most of them. But one reason many girls keep it on the down-low is because they're afraid their boyfriends will abandon them. That fear exists because many guys have done exactly that. But for the rest of us fellas, the ones who would never do that, it's a bummer. Guess it's up to us to change people's minds about this stereotype. Fellas, back me up here. Talk to your girlfriends, and let them know you'll be there if and when they need you.

Coming from the female perspective, I think your girlfriend was well within her rights to wait to tell you.

I mean, think about it: Figuring out what you're going to do about something this huge is hard enough when you're only thinking about yourself. Bringing someone else into the equation can make things much more difficult. By talking to you about it, she would've risked getting pressure from you about what to do.

And while she didn't get pregnant on her own, being pregnant affects her body and her future—or lack of one—way more than it affects yours.

No matter how cool or how understanding of a boyfriend you may be, you'll never know exactly how that feels. She made the choice that was best for her. And that's her legal and moral right.

he should've been told BEFORE she made that decision. it was his baby, too. he should have at least been told. that was so wrong of her! —lexis

it is the father's right to know about the pregnancy, but the decision to have an abortion is totally up to the girl. —hanch

class that abstinence is their only protection option.

same–sex stuff

chapter **8**

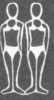

No matter what your sexual orientation is, it's not wrong. Period.

No matter what your sexual orientation is, it's yours. Period.

And no matter what your sexual orientation is, you're not the only one. Period.

Figuring out who you are and who you love isn't as easy as everyone wants it to be. It's a long, strange trip that we all have to go through. For some, it's longer and stranger than it is for others. That's what we're gonna talk about in this chapter.

Feeling like yours is longer and stranger than you can handle? Reach out. In your community, there might be an organization that can help you. In your school, there might be a counselor who can lend an ear. On-line, there are plenty of places to find support. Even in your family, there might be someone you can lean on when you need it. Look around. You don't have to go through it alone.

my crush is gay

I've been in love with this guy for three years now, and last night I found out that he's gay!

I don't know how I could be so stupid. He doesn't act gay, and I never noticed it.

The real problem is my friend just told him I like him. Now I feel like a complete fool and don't know what to do! Please help me—I'm feeling so lost, confused, and depressed now.

—RAVEON1

DEAR RAVEON1,

Oops. :-) Okay, I know you're bugging, but as of right now, you can officially start to chill.

Why? Because you didn't do anything stupid or foolish. I mean, how were you supposed to know? You say he doesn't act gay, but whatever you're thinking of when you say that probably applies to, like, oh, 1 percent of gay people. Stereotypes like acting flamboyant or feminine or whatever just aren't true. Looks like you learned that lesson.

Don't worry about what he thinks of you now. I mean, yeah, he's not going to go out with you, and you have to deal with that. But I'm sure he doesn't think you're a weirdo. He's probably flattered.

And when it comes right down to it, he's got much bigger issues to deal with at this point. So you, Raveon1, oughta think about just being his friend and giving him a hand.

fiona says

Although you feel like you've just made this major discovery about him, the truth is, really nothing about him has changed. He is still the awesome guy you thought he was before.

He just won't ever want to go out with you.

But that's okay. You can get past that. If you thought he'd make an awesome boyfriend, he's probably an awesome friend to have.

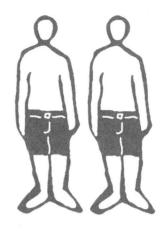

And don't feel too stupid for not knowing his orientation. Although it's wrong, in our society it's assumed that everyone's straight. Hmmm, reminds me of that thing my fifth-grade teacher used to always say: "When you assume, you make an ass outta u and me."

I can almost guarantee that he will want to be your friend unless he is just like some huge snob or something. —honeybee

Ever seen the movie Clueless??? Well, if not, you should watch it. I think the way Cher handled the situation was perfect! —forsythia

she's trying to
make me straight

Okay, here's the deal. I came out to a really good friend a few weeks ago. She's a girl, and I'm a guy. I know that she liked me as more than a friend a couple of years ago, but she said she was over that.

Anyway, she was really cool when I first told her—but lately she's getting really flirty again, saying how we should hook up and she can change me back. I like her a lot—but not like that. I need her to shut up.

Help!

—ANNOYED

DEAR ANNOYED,

tucker says

I assume you've already tried, "Shut up."

I guess it didn't take.

Your next tactic? Take a break from each other.

Sounds like she really digs you, man, but she's also clearly confused. Probably because when you told her you were gay, you went from a possibility to a total impossibility. You already knew it was never going to happen, so you had an advantage. She was still holding out hope.

Her first reaction was to be really cool, to be your friend. That proves that she'll get over it eventually. I predict your friendship will survive, but you both need time apart. She needs it so she can get over you. And you, my friend, have enough to deal with as it is.

Yeah, I agree. It sounds like you two definitely need some time apart.

Because in my experience, the quickest and least traumatic way to get over someone is to avoid seeing them altogether. You know, the whole outta-sight, outta-mind gig. . . . It's really the best thing for both of you.

So tell your friend that you need some space, and then take a break from each other. (A good two months or so without any contact should do the trick.) And then, after the cooling-down period, when you guys hang out again, make it clear to her that there's no way that you're "changing back."

You're not, like, going through a phase. You've realized something important about who you really are, and that's not going to change. Tell her that your sexual orientation is part of you—and she can either be a friend and accept you—as is—or forget about being in your life.

> **HAVE YOU EVER CRUSHED ON SOMEONE OF THE SAME GENDER?**
> Yeah, all the time: 4%
> Yeah, once or twice: 13%
> Never: 71%
> No answer: 12%

if she was any kind of friend then she would respect your choice and your feelings. you need to give this girl a piece of your mind.

—angieG

dude, u should be flattered she's hot for u. —rand

am i **bisexual?**

I've got a question burning in my head. . . . See, I've been thinking about this. I'm into guys & everything, but lately I've been thinking that I would fool around with a girl. The only thing is, that's all I would do with a girl: Fool around. I wouldn't want a relationship or anything. I don't wanna sound slutty, but does this make me bisexual?
Thanks!

—LORELEI

DEAR LORELEI,
tucker says

Nah, probably not.

Everyone has thoughts and even fantasies about people of the same gender. Everyone. Even all those people who deny it.

People freak out about it, though, because all of a sudden they start to think that those feelings actually define who they are. But they don't. They're fantasies, plain and simple.

Even when people have real, full-on same-sex experiences, it doesn't necessarily mean that they'll start living their lives that way. People experiment with all kinds of stuff before figuring out who they are. So don't bug.

But think about this: If you were bisexual, would that be so bad?

Later.

and bisexual youth are more than four times more likely to attempt

fiona says

It's totally normal to think about what it would be like to make out with another girl. Like Tucker said, everyone fantasizes about what it'd be like. Everyone.

I mean, why do you think Ally McBeal's ratings go through the roof every time Ally swaps spit with one of her female coworkers? It's intriguing. People are curious about what it would be like for themselves.

So there's no reason to get freaked out. Thinking about other girls is natural. And it doesn't mean that you're bisexual. It means you're human.

i make out with my best girlfriend all the time. it's fun. —lizlova

Isn't everyone bisexual? Not me, of course. :-)—klad

should i **come out**
to my best friend?

Help me, please. I am a girl, and I know that I like girls. The only problem is that I'm attracted to my best friend—but my friend is straight. It's really bugging me, and I know that if I tell my friend how I feel, she'll not only freak out—she'll tell all my other friends, too. What do I do? I can't keep this inside me forever.

Thanks,

—FRIENDS FOREVER

DEAR FRIENDS,

If you know that your friend is straight and very likely to freak, you definitely shouldn't tell her that you're attracted to her. As messed up as it is, a lot of people who are otherwise very cool still can't handle homosexuality. Although they have no reason to be weirded out, they sometimes feel threatened by people who aren't straight. So if I were you, I'd keep your crush on your friend quiet.

But while you shouldn't confess your crush to your friend, you should talk to someone. You've got some deep stuff on your mind—and you can't keep it bottled up inside. If you can't talk to your friends or your family, you may want to look for support from gay groups.

The National Youth Advocacy Coalition (NYAC) is a national clearinghouse for info on issues concerning gay, lesbian, bisexual, and transgender (GLBT) youth and maintains

sex.—Limp Bizkit As far as I am concerned, sex ruins almost every-a database of 4,000 support groups, community-based agencies, and GLBT youth advocates. For info, e-mail nyac@nyacyouth.org or visit www.nyacyouth.org. Or call the Gay and Lesbian National Hotline (888-THE-GLNH) toll free—it offers free and anonymous information, referrals, and counseling.

The important thing to keep in mind is that even though your friend may not understand what you're going through or there aren't other gays in your town, you're not alone. There are other people who will be there for you—and you should reach out to them.

tucker says

The thing about coming out is, you have to be brave, but you also have to be smart and realistic. Sometimes full disclosure just isn't in your best interest. Especially when you're still struggling with this stuff yourself.

You need to talk to people you can seriously trust, not people who you think might bug out. Does that mean talking to people who aren't your close friends or family members? Yep. Anyone who loves you has a much bigger chance of going house.

Talk to someone who knows what they're talking about first. Anyone from the places Fiona mentioned will listen. They won't judge you. And they'll help you figure out how to get support from people you love.

friends love friends no matter what. if your friend can't deal, she's not a friend. —peeka

Forget what people say about you. . . . It is what is inside that counts in all of us. —lindsylu

thing.—Sandra Bernhard Lift my days . . . light up my nights.—U2

my best friend just came out! now what?

Yikes! Your best friend just told you she's gay. Or she thinks she might be gay. Or she's attracted to someone of the same sex. Here are some tips for handling the big news:

DON'T FREAK (in front of your friend)
But if you know you need some time to deal, let your friend know. Then go freak somewhere else and get it out of your system.

BE THERE
Make it very clear, straight up, that you care and that you'll be friends no matter what, even if you don't quite identify. Then say it again, just in case. Okay, one more time. There.

ASK LOTS OF QUESTIONS
Asking how your friend feels and how she is dealing will let her know you care. But don't expect your friend to know all the answers. After all, just because she's gay doesn't mean she knows everything about being gay. Your friend is just learning, too. The most impossible question you could ask is, "Why are you gay?"

FIND OUT MORE
Learn as much as you can about your friend's situation. Read, talk, listen, watch—find out anything and everything you can about gay and lesbian life. Oh, and don't find out about it from the Springer show or some hoo-has in your school who have no idea what they're talking about. Find out from someone or something that knows. A good place to start is www.glsen.org.

KEEP IT QUIET

Agree to keep everything under wraps and mean it. You must not tell anyone unless your friend specifically tells you it's okay. This is NOT GOSSIP. . . . It's too serious for that. You've seen the harassment; you've heard the horror stories. Don't put your friend in a position to be one of the victims.

TELL 'EM HOW YOU FEEL

Once you've given yourself time to absorb it all, talk to your friend about how all this makes you feel. Tell him/her that you're in it together, but you need support, too.

DON'T OBSESS

Your friend is not your GAY friend now; she is still just your friend. So the gay thing doesn't have to take over your relationship. Don't forget about the rest.

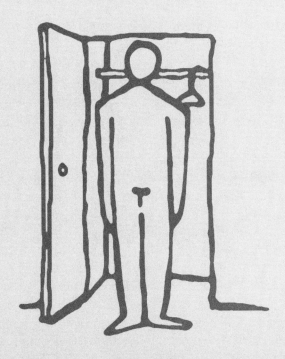

i'm gay and
i'm crushing

Okay, so I'm gay. And there is this really hot guy that I really want to talk to. I know that he is "bisexual," but I have never talked to him before! I don't know how I should approach him! I have a friend that is trying to help me become more blunt, but I don't know if I could be blunt enough to just walk up to him and say, "Hey, you're hot—do you want to hook up sometime?" Ya know?? So please HELP!!
Thanx,

—OVERCAST

DEAR OVERCAST,

First of all, you sound like a confident guy to me. I mean, comfortable with your orientation.

That means you're pretty strong, know what I mean? So asking someone out will be way easier than you think.

Still, I don't think you should walk up and say, "Hey, you're hot—let's hook up." That, my friend, is a little bit too blunt, and he'll think you're a freak. Instead, see if he wants to grab a coffee, or go shopping for CDs, or whatever. Talk about something other than hooking up, you know? Soon enough you'll catch a vibe and you'll know whether it could go anywhere.

If it doesn't, don't get too down.

Good luck.

It 's getting laid when you 're not famous that takes some talent.—Kevin

fiona says

No one likes to think of themselves as a big, ol' piece o' meat.

And if you approach this guy and tell him that you wanna get busy, that's how he's going to feel. And there's a very large possibility that he will be turned off by that.

Unless he's only out for some easy nookie, too.

Not that you said you just want action. But that's what he'll think unless you chill a bit. And who knows, you might not even wanna hook up with this guy once you start talking.

Be careful. I'm gay and I hit on a friend of mine who freaked. Now we don't speak. —dal

You're like me, Overcast. I'm not gay, but I don't have the nerve to ask out the girl that I like, either. —ScottyX

how do i meet
other lesbians?

I'm a 16-year-old lesbian, but I don't know how to find the right one for me. Every time I get into a relationship, it goes bad. Do you have any advice? Where can I meet a great girl?

—LONELY LESBIAN

DEAR LONELY LESBIAN,

Hey, first of all, props on being so aware and confident about your sexuality. You're way ahead of the rest of us.

Second of all, it looks like you've discovered that it's just as hard to find "the right one" when you're gay as it is for anyone else. Sorry, no answers here. That's, like, the impossible question.

Third, it sucks that you don't feel like you can just use the same method everyone else does for finding dates: asking people out. I mean, you totally run the risk of getting harassed if you ask someone out and they turn out to be really mean. That sucks major. Again, props for dealing.

Okay, so where's the perfect girl hiding out? Well, you could always check out local gay and lesbian youth support groups for possible dates. I mean, sure . . . they help you deal and all, but let's face it . . . those hangouts gotta have some major hooking up going on. Just like any other youth group, know what I'm saying? If you haven't been there, look it up and go say hey. Worth a shot, right?

Did that already? Well, why not pursue some of your own

interests, and see who it leads to? I mean, if you're into dancing, take a class! If you're into sports, play 'em! If you're into theater, get a part in a play! Seriously—it may not seem the clearest path to a significant other, but hey . . . you never know who you'll meet. Besides . . . if you're there, who's to say the girl of your dreams won't be, too?

Good luck!

If finding someone special were as easy as going to the right club or concert or whatever, the world's problems would be solved. Heck, I wouldn't even be at work right now—I'd be there, hooking up with a sensitive indie rock boy with an art degree.

Oh, but whoops, that's my dream person. Now back to yours.

So where is she? Who knows? But keep your head up—she is out there. And by the way, the whole dating game will probably get easier once you're out living on your own. It always does.

Hang in there!

I have major respect for this girl for being comfortable with her sexuality already. Good luck. —graf

Girl—go on-line. Go to a lesbian chat room and talk to the girls in there! —queendawg

have been 80 documented cases of men with two penises.

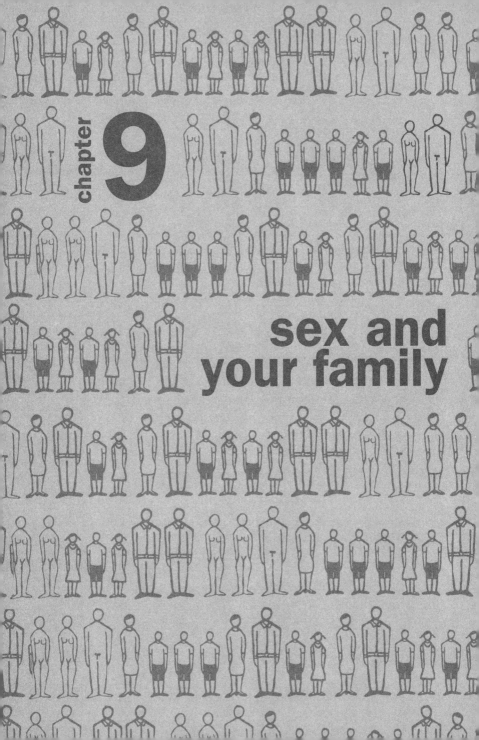

chapter **9**

sex and
your family

What is it about sex that makes even the most incredibly understanding parents go all freaky?

Maybe it's because no matter what age you are, your parents (and sometimes your older siblings, too) still think of you as about five years old. So thinking about you having sex or fooling around is about as frightening for them as, well, thinking about *them* having sex is for you. Possibly even worse (if you can imagine that).

Whatever the reason, talking to your family about sex can be anywhere from embarrassing to downright pointless. So it's up to you to decide what you can go to them for (relationship issues, making gyno appointments, stuff like that) and what you can't. But before you make that decision, check yourself. Are you underestimating them? I mean, when you get past the awkwardness and everything else, is it possible that they might actually offer you some sound advice? If so, you might want to reconsider. If not, you need to start looking somewhere else for answers. But make sure you get those answers somewhere.

my parents **suck**

I hate my parents. They are being so unfair! See, they let my brother, who's 17, and his girlfriend hang out alone all the time. They even went camping together! But they won't let me (I'm 15) and my boyfriend do anything!

It sucks! My boyfriend and I aren't even allowed to be alone in my room together. And I'm not allowed to stay out past ten on the weekend. But my brother always has his GF over and comes home whenever he feels like it.

I'm so sick of it! It's not even like my BF and I do that much!

—JESSI

DEAR JESSI,

They're keeping you on a tight leash, huh? And you're wondering why.

I bet if you asked your dad, he'd say something like, "You can't be alone with boys. They only have one thing on their mind. Believe me, I know."

I bet if you asked your mom, she'd say something like, "Boys are after one thing and one thing only. Believe me, I know."

They're doing it, Jessi, because they love you. And in its own strange way, it kinda makes a little sense. And who knows? They may have more information than you do.

Bottom line: Tough noogies. They're still the bosses, and until you're up and outta there, they call the shots. In the meantime, prove you're responsible by following all their

During foreplay, a woman's breasts can increase in size up to 25%.

rules exactly perfectly. They'll start to notice, and maybe they'll even relax things a little.

tucker says

Yeah, I know you're tired of hearing the usual "their roof, their rules" spiel. But unfortunately, that's the way it is. Unless you plan on dropping outta school and supporting yourself. Which I do not recommend at all.

You need your parents. And what they're doing—annoying as it is—is for your own good. (Yeah, no one likes to hear that one, either.) But seriously, you're 15—and that just happens to be the age when many girls have sex for the first time. And every year about 1 million American girls get pregnant. Get it? They don't want you to become another statistic.

And I don't, either. So even if you do find a way to get around your parents' ultrastrict rules, if you and your boyfriend do start getting hot 'n' heavy, you gotta make sure to protect yourself. Not just from pregnancy, but from STDs, too.

Oh, and one more thing about your parents: Did they allow your brother to hang out with girls when he was 15? If not, then they may not be as unfair as you think. If they did, they may be subjecting you to a double standard, which really sucks. But unfortunately, you have to live with it for now. Try talking to them about it. And maybe, by the time you're 17, they'll be cool.

Following their rules exactly works. That's what I've been doing, and I've been able to hang out more with my boyfriend. —babygrll

Ask them if u can invite him over for dinner so they can get a good impression of him. —jazzoo

It'll feel all right. Well, I wanna make your motor run.—Meatloaf

my mom doesn't believe that i
haven't done it

I am a 15-, about to be 16-year-old virgin. For some reason, my mother doesn't believe that I am a virgin. I don't know why. Is it because she doesn't trust me or what?

What should I do? How can I get my mom to believe that I am a virgin?

And if she still doesn't believe me, should I just go ahead and do it? A lot of boys have asked me to have sex with them, but I've refused them all.

—STILL A V

fiona says

DEAR STILL A V,

Um, why do you care so much?

I mean, sure, what your parents think about you is important—but if your mom refuses to believe that you're still a virgin, there really isn't much you can do to about it.

At one point, my mom was sure that I had a tattoo—even though I didn't. I kept denying it, but she wouldn't believe me. Finally it blew over. And thank God because it was really annoying that she didn't believe me.

And who knows why your mom doesn't believe you? Maybe she doesn't trust you. Or perhaps she thinks you're just at that age when many people start having sex, so she's just assuming that you've done it, too.

The important thing is that you know the truth. You don't need to prove anything to her—and you shouldn't just do it to do it, either.

The occurrence of intercourse in the U.S. peaks in July. Every time I

Like Fiona said, the important thing is that you know the truth. But as we all know, that doesn't make this situation any less annoying.

I think you really need to challenge her on this one. I'm sort of guessing that you haven't sat down and talked about it, heart-to-heart, but that's exactly what you need to do. So go on, have a full-on conversation with her. Tell her, once and for all, that you're being honest and that it hurts you that she doesn't believe you. Point out that there's no reason for her to doubt you (right? RIGHT?) and that you're telling the straight-up truth.

Don't start the conversation all angry. Sit down, speak calmly and intelligently, and she'll have to pay attention. And then let it lie. Even if she doesn't ultimately believe you, maybe at least she will understand that you've figured out that your body is yours and that those decisions are yours to make.

Oh, and while we're on the your-body-is-yours tip, of all the bad reasons to "just go ahead and do it," probably the worst one is because your mother thinks you already did. That's like giving her control over your body. Don't go there.

Regardless of what we do or say, moms just can't get it through their skulls that we aren't as wild as we may seem to be. —lilnotphil

Tell her that it really hurt your feelings when she said that she didn't believe you. —natasha

think about the love we make it makes my heart sink.—Sisqo I want to

my **mom knows**
i'm not a virgin

I am not a virgin, and my mother knows, and we are all cool with it. The problem is that since my boyfriend and I broke up, I've been going to a lot of parties and meeting guys.

Now my mom automatically thinks that I am a slut and have been sleeping around with people. I haven't!! I have told her this, but she says she is worried about me and now probably won't let me party anymore.

What can I do to let her know that I am not a slut and get back her respect and trust?

—HELP

tucker says

DEAR HELP,

Okay, you're gonna hate me for saying this, but . . . it's time to sit down and have a heart-to-heart with Joe. Joe Mama, that is.

See, not that I'm a parent or anything, but I can imagine that it would be easier for me to deal with having a sexually active son or daughter if I knew who she was being sexually active with. When your mother knew there were limits to your activity (in other words, she knew exactly who you were getting busy with), she had a little less to worry about.

But now, since you're a free agent, she has more to bug out about. See what I mean?

Your only hope? To sit her down and talk to her about how responsible and trustworthy you are. (You are both of those things, right?) Hopefully she'll get the pic.

If she does understand, you'll have a better relationship with her than ever. If she doesn't, tough noogies. You're living in her house for the next few years, and bummer though it may be, she calls the shots.

fiona says

Yep. The only possible way through this situation IS to talk to your mother. Like the mature, responsible, non-slutty young adult that you are.

Make it clear to your mom that you can be trusted to be responsible about sex. Let her know that just because you did the deed with your ex, it doesn't mean that you're now rearin' to give it up to just anyone. And while you're at it, don't forget to mention that her assuming that you're a big hoochie is, well, kinda hurtful.

So talk to your mom—and fight for your right to party! Good luck.

Don't lie about anything because that will only make things worse in the end. —I rule

Instead of child to parent, talk to her adult to adult. Communication works if you're willing to understand their point of view also. . . . —Canu

164

they wanna get with
my sister

My sister is a freshman this year, and all of my friends seem to want her.

She's going to prom with one of my friends who's known to be a huge player. She is on every junior and senior guy's wish list. It kills me 'cause I'm a guy, and I know how we think.

My sister isn't Miss Innocent, either, and I don't want her having sex with one of them. But she's mad at me for being overprotective!

—RICKY

DEAR RICKY,

It's totally normal to be overprotective of your little sis. Especially 'cause it sounds like your friends are, well, a bunch of dogs.

But the thing is, you can't control your sister's sex life. You can lecture her all you want. You can even tell your friends to keep their hands off her. But ultimately, what your sis does or doesn't do is her decision. And if she wants to have sex, she'll do it—whether you like it or not.

All you can do is try to tell her that the guy she's going to prom with has a rep and that she should be careful. But believe it or not, by letting her know that you're looking out for her, you're already helping her.

tucker says

Does your little sister even really know or understand exactly what you're protecting her from? I bet if you sit down and give her the deal, straight up (and be graphic, dude . . . don't candy coat it), she might not be so mad.

I remember when I was like six years old, everyone was always all, "No!" when I wanted to jump off the swing set. But I still wanted to do it . . . and the fact that everyone kept saying no made me want to do it more. Then this girl in my class, Bessie, jumped off—and broke both of her arms. She had two casts for the rest of the school year. That's when I understood.

If you want your sister to understand why you're being so overprotective, you've got to give her the nitty-gritty details. (Tell her you love her and all that, too.)

Oh, and while you're at it, tell your friends that they need to respect your sister, period. No discussion.

After doing all that, Ricky, you've gotta do the hardest thing of all: Sit back and let her live her life.

i totally wish that i had an older brother like you. nobody really cares about what happens between me and guys and i think that it's great that you're looking out for her. —erikaderika

Just don't be all "I told you so" if something does happen.
—mymy

should i **tell my mom** i'm sexually active?

> I have had sex, and I don't want my mom to find out or she will kill me.
>   What should I do? Should I tell her and listen to her lecture or just keep it secret?
>
> —ME

DEAR ME,

It all depends.

If you truly think she might be able to give you some answers, or support, or deep wisdom, then yeah, I'd tell her.

But if you're sure she's just going to go straight-up ballistic, I'd find someone else to talk to about it.

See, in a perfect world, it'd be great to have open, honest, rational communication about sex with your parents. But that usually only happens in health class pamphlet land. Real life requires both sides to be open, honest, and rational. And let's face it—parents can be just as messed up and unhelpful when talking about sex as anyone else.

Getting in trouble for having sex won't help the situation. What you need is to sit down and talk with someone who knows what they're talking about, who won't get mad at you, and who will have some answers. Is that your mother? If it is, right on. Go have a chat. But if it isn't, you gotta find someone else. Someone like a counselor at school (don't gag; it's not that bad). Or another relative (got a cool aunt or uncle?). Or

an older friend (much older, please, not just a grade ahead of you). Or a local youth group leader.

Sounds to me like you're jonesing to talk to someone. Look around—you'll find 'em.

fiona says

It sounds to me like you've already made your decision.

You know that your mom would freak if she knew you were having sex. And you don't need a freak-out or a lecture—because let's face it, you're going to do what you want to do no matter what your mom or anyone else says.

So no matter what, make sure you take care of yourself. You can get condoms and birth control pills from a local clinic like Planned Parenthood. You can also get tested for STDs there. And their staff can answer any specific questions you have about your reproductive health.

Hey! if i were u, i wouldn't tell my mom i was having sex 'cause it's really none of her business. —raykwan

She just wants to keep you safe—
it's her job . . . so if she gets sketched out a little,
that's okay. She's the mom . . . tell her. —dandi

were spinning into darkness; the earth was on fire.—Pink Floyd

the
talk

Ugh, The Talk. No one wants to have it. Not even your parents.

But The Talk can be a seriously good thing. It lets your parents know what's up with you—which can help reaffirm their trust in you and put their minds at ease (depending on what you are and aren't doing).

It's also one of the best ways you can get the support you need from someone you trust and who you know has your best interests in mind. Whether you have to go to the doctor for an exam, get info about birth control, or tackle a more serious issue—like pregnancy—sometimes it's helpful to have an adult on your side.

So how do you get things started?

First, figure out which parent is easier to talk to. Maybe you're more comfortable talking about some subjects with your mom and others with your dad. The important thing is to be able to talk to someone if you need to.

Warm 'em up. If out of the blue you blurt out, "I wanna go on the pill," or, "I have to go to the gyno," your parents may be taken aback. Get them used to talking with you about semi-embarrassing issues before spilling anything major. Start with small stuff—or get them talking by asking them about themselves.

Of course, when it comes to bigger issues, like, "My girlfriend is pregnant," or, "I think I might have an

STD. What do I do?" it's
impossible to fully
prepare someone. But
if you're used to talk-
ing to your parents
about sex, it'll
make it that much
easier to commu-
nicate with them
when you really
need to.

   If your par-
ents seem too
busy or too
embarrassed to talk when
you bring sex stuff up casu-
ally, then set a time to talk.
That way, they'll know
you've got serious stuff on
your mind and will probably
make more of an effort to
pay attention to what you
have to say.

   Remember, no matter
how much you think your
parents will freak out at the
mere mention of sex, if you
need their help, you should
ask for it. And usually they'll
be more willing to support
you than you think.

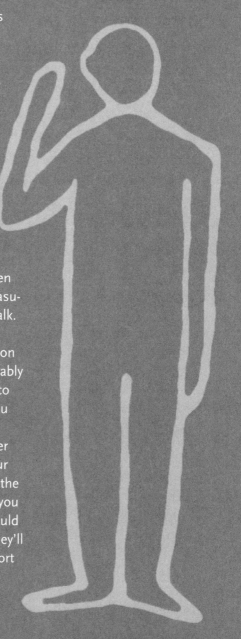

conclusion

Okay, there you have it—our answers to your most burning sex questions.

We've tried to drop the science on everything you wanna know about. But of course, no matter how similar the scenarios in this book are to what you may be dealing with, your experiences are, well, unique.

So what do you do if the situation you're in is different from what we've covered in this book?

Use your head. (No, not that one!) Sure, sex may seem confusing and all-consuming at times. But it doesn't have to be. Really, when it comes to sex—just like when it comes to anything else—you've got choices. Lots of 'em.

And when it comes to your body, your feelings, and your future, you have to make the choices that are best for you and only you. Not best for your boyfriend. Not best for your girlfriend. Not best for your friends or even your family. Just you. So determine where you stand on the issues, don't give in to pressure to do anything you don't want to do, don't make any rash decisions, and be prepared for all the consequences of your actions.

The bottom line: Be smart, be safe, and stick with your decisions—and you'll be fine.

Take care of yourself,

tucker and fiona

TICKER SOURCE LIST:

PP. 101-104: Centers for Disease Control and Prevention, 1999.

P. 113: National Center for Chronic Disease Prevention and Health Promotion, 1999.

PP.113-114: Kaiser Family Foundation, 1998.

PP. 114-115: Global Summary of the AIDS Epidemic, 1999.

P. 118: www.itsyoursexlife.com.

PP.119-120: Centers for Disease Control and Prevention, 1997.

P. 126: www.itsyoursexlife.com.

PP. 127-128: www.plannedparenthood.org.

pp.137-139: www.plannedparenthood.org.

PP. 144-145: Making Schools Safe for Gay and Lesbian Youth: Report of the Massachusetts Governor's Commission on Gay and Lesbian Youth, 1993.

PP. 145-146: The Center for Disease Control and Prevention and The Massachusetts Department of Education, The Massachusetts Youth Risk Behavior Survey, 1997.